$29.00

ASSESSMENT
IN PSYCHOTHERAPY

ASSESSMENT
IN PSYCHOTHERAPY

edited by
Judy Cooper and Helen Alfillé

With contributions by members of the
Clinical Service of the British Association of Psychotherapists

Foreword by
Margret Tonnesmann

London
KARNAC BOOKS

First published in 1998 by
H. Karnac (Books) Ltd.
58 Gloucester Road
London SW7 4QY

British Library Cataloging in Publication Data

A C.I.P. record for this book is available from the British Library.

ISBN 1 85575 158 5

Edited, designed, and produced by Communication Crafts

Printed in Great Britain by BPC Wheatons Ltd, Exeter

10 9 8 7 6 5 4 3 2 1

Canst thou not minister to a mind diseas'd,
Pluck from the memory a rooted sorrow,
Raze out the written troubles of the brain,
And with some . . . antidote
Cleanse the stuff'd bosom of that perilous stuff
Which weighs upon the heart?

Shakespeare, "Macbeth", Act V, Scene iii: 40-45

Know then thyself, presume not God to scan,
The proper study of Mankind is Man.

Alexander Pope, "An Essay on Man", II, 1–2

CONTENTS

FOREWORD by Margret Tonnesmann   ix

PREFACE   xiii

CONTRIBUTORS   xv

Introduction
Judy Cooper and Helen Alfillé   1

CHAPTER ONE
Assessment for psychoanalytic psychotherapy:
an overview of the literature
Ruth Berkowitz   7

CHAPTER TWO
Where referrals come from
and some links with general practice
Judith Barnard   35

CHAPTER THREE
The difference between diagnosis and assessment
in psychoanalytic psychotherapy
    Anne Tyndale   47

CHAPTER FOUR
Once-weekly or more intensive therapy
    Judy Cooper and Helen Alfillé   63

CHAPTER FIVE
The significance of the opening story
    Arna Davis   69

CHAPTER SIX
The assessment consultation
    Aslan Mordecai and Danuta Waydenfeld   87

CHAPTER SEVEN
Transference and countertransference
in the assessment consultation
    Mary Rosalind Stumpfl   107

CHAPTER EIGHT
Boundaries and difficulties in assessment
    Philip Hewitt   115

CHAPTER NINE
Contraindications
for psychodynamic psychotherapy
    Mira Malovic-Yeeles   125

Conclusions
    Judy Cooper and Helen Alfillé   135

REFERENCES   139

INDEX   149

FOREWORD

Margret Tonnesmann

W hen Donald Winnicott was asked who could benefit from psychoanalytic therapy, he said that psycho-analytic psychotherapy was for those who need it, who want it, and who can make use of it.

At the end of the last century, Sigmund Freud devised what is known as the psychoanalytic setting for the treatment of those patients who suffered from psychoneurotic disorders. They had defended themselves against awareness of conflictual wishes and thoughts, which had led to various symptom formations. Patients who needed psychoanalytic psychotherapy as available at that time were those who suffered from often crippling psychoneurotic symptoms.

Those who wanted to undergo treatment had to be highly motivated to accept a therapeutic procedure that involved ex-periences of unpleasant and often painful emotions. Already at that time, it became questionable whether it was good enough to be sent for treatment by relatives or friends. The case of Dora (Freud, 1905e [1901]) seems a telling example of a patient whose motivation was not good enough to see her through the full course of therapy.

Patients who could make use of therapy were those who could follow the "basic rule". This meant that they had to report all thoughts and feelings that they experienced during the sessions, and the analyst listened with "free hovering attention" to understand the unconscious content of their patients' communications. In time, the repressed psychic material that was assumed to originate from unresolved conflicts of the oedipal phase of development became available again and was re-experienced in the transference relationship to the analyst. By interpreting these events and by making links between the present and the past, the analyst brought them to the awareness of the patient who could now understand the meaning that his symptom conveyed.

Only those patients who had a strong enough ego and were of reasonable intelligence were regarded as suitable. In cases of doubt, a trial period of therapy would be arranged before patient and analyst decided about its continuation.

Assessment of patients' suitability to benefit from psychoanalytic therapy was relatively straightforward: it included diagnosis, assessment of the patient's ego strength, and also assessment of the sincerity of motivation for treatment.

With the development of psychoanalytic theory, in particular of concepts of infant development, the scope for patients who could benefit from psychoanalytic therapy has widened. It is not any longer assumed that only patients who suffer from psychoneuroses can benefit, but also those who present with a variety of symptoms due to conflicts and traumata during early development that had left their mark in distortions and arrests of further development. The emphasis has changed towards regarding the quality of infant care and early object relations as essential factors in mental and psychic health.

Psychoanalytic psychotherapy can now also aim at helping patients to gain insight into their difficulties of relating to others and into their experiences of a lack of meaningful emotional living and inner emptiness, so that they can grow and move towards a better integration.

The one-person psychology of Freud and his early followers who understood the patients' transferences as an intrapsychic phenomenon has changed into a two-person psychology (Balint, 1950; Rickman, 1951). The patient as well as the psychotherapist

are subjectively involved in the interaction of the therapeutic process. The analyst's countertransference responses to the patient's
communications are seen as an essential tool for understanding
the patient–therapist relationship. It depends on the theoretical
orientation of the individual therapist whether she conceives of
the interactions as the patient's projective identifications of part of
the self or of an object from his inner world or as a revival of the
his early object relationships with a facilitating environment that
may have failed at vital stages of early development and so had
left its mark on his emotional and mental health.

With this development of psychoanalytic theory and its concomitant changes in the understanding of the therapeutic process,
the task of the assessor has fundamentally changed. The consultation now aims at creating a milieu in which both patient and
therapist are emotionally engaged. The patient will experience an
encounter with the assessor in which he may feel understood,
whereas the assessor will use his countertransference responses as
an important tool for his professional judgement. It is the patient
who has an opportunity to decide afresh whether he wants
psychotherapy, and it is the therapist who will have to decide
whether the patient needs psychotherapy.

Whether the patient will be able to use psychotherapy evolves
from the reactions of the patient to the assessor's interventions,
but it is often also apparent in the way that the patient communicates his difficulties in living as he would wish to live his life. This
is variously described as being psychologically minded or as the
patient's ability to engage in a therapeutic alliance.

Diagnosis of illness is only important at the borders—for
example, if the patient is floridly psychotic or acutely suicidal
and needs medical care in the narrow sense of the term, or if the
patient shows a tendency to violent acting-out. It is the assessor's
encounter with the patient that also enables him to decide
whether the patient is best served with individual psychoanalytic
psychotherapy or whether he may benefit more from other
analytically informed forms of therapy like group, family, or
marital psychotherapy.

The patient brings his hopes and his fears to the assessment
consultation, the assessor his skills as an experienced psychoanalytic psychotherapist based on his particular theoretical

orientation. But both patient and assessor also meet as the individuals they are, which means that every assessment consultation evolves as a unique intersubjective encounter.

This book has collected together contributions written by experienced psychotherapists, who present their individual ways of conducting assessment consultations and come to decisions about whether the patient needs psychotherapy, wants it, and can make use of it.

PREFACE

This book was conceived by the Editors following the realization that the assessments done by members of the Clinical Service of the British Association of Psychotherapists (BAP), since it formally came into being in January 1983, formed a considerable core of knowledge and experience. Between us, we have done literally hundreds of assessments and have subsequently referred many of these patients on for psychoanalytic psychotherapy. The contributors to this book are all members of the Clinical Service assessment team for individual adult psychotherapy. There is also a Child and Adolescent Clinic in the BAP, which has its own assessment procedure. We hope that the sharing of our joint expertise may be helpful for all those therapists who inevitably find themselves faced with conducting an assessment, often with very little experience and few guidelines.

While there is overall cohesion in the way that assessments are conducted and referrals subsequently made, there are differences in the terminology, partly due to the two orientations—psychoanalytic and Jungian—in the BAP. Although there is a distinction between psychoanalytic psychotherapy and psychoanalysis, for the purpose of this book the terms have for the most part been used interchangeably, except where it was necessary for a distinction to be made.

The Editors would like to thank Judith Lawrence, Secretary of the BAP, for her involvement and interest in the Clinical Service from its inception. Also, Linda Farley, librarian of the BAP, for all her generous help. We are most grateful to Cesare Sacerdoti for his creative criticism and to Graham Sleight and Eric and Klara King for their enthusiasm and support, which has encouraged us in our efforts to produce this book.

CONTRIBUTORS

Helen Alfillé
Member of the British Association of Psychotherapists,
Psychoanalytic Psychotherapy Section. In private practice in
London.

Judith Barnard MD
Associate Member of the British Association of Psychotherapists,
Psychoanalytic Psychotherapy Section. In private practice in
London. Formerly in general practice.

Ruth Berkowitz PhD
Member of the British Association of Psychotherapists,
Psychoanalytic Psychotherapy Section. In private practice in
London. Also trained as a family therapist at the Tavistock
Centre.

Judy Cooper
Member of the British Association of Psychotherapists,
Psychoanalytic Psychotherapy Section. Author: *Speak of Me as I
Am: The Life and Work of Masud Khan* (London: Karnac Books,

1993). Co-editor: *Narcissistic Wounds: Clinical Perspectives* (London: Whurr Publishers, 1995). In private practice in London.

Arna Davis
Member of the British Association of Psychotherapists, Jungian Analytic Section. In private practice in Hertfordshire. Has published in professional journals.

Philip Hewitt
Member of the British Association of Psychotherapists, Psychoanalytic Psychotherapy Section. Consultant to organizations working with addicts and in private practice in London.

Mira Malovic-Yeeles MD
Associate Member of the British Association of Psychotherapists, Jungian Analytic Section. Psychiatrist at the Warneford Hospital, Oxford and in private practice in Oxford. Has published in several professional journals.

Aslan Mordecai PhD
Member of the British Association of Psychotherapists, Psychoanalytic Psychotherapy Section. In private practice in London. Associate Fellow of the British Psychological Society.

Mary Rosalind Stumpfl
Member of the British Association of Psychotherapists, Psychoanalytic Psychotherapy Section. In private practice in London.

Anne Tyndale
Member of the British Association of Psychotherapists, Psychoanalytic Psychotherapy Section. In private practice in Brighton.

Danuta Waydenfeld
Member of the British Association of Psychotherapists, Psychoanalytic Psychotherapy Section. In private practice in London.

ASSESSMENT IN PSYCHOTHERAPY

Introduction

Judy Cooper and Helen Alfillé

> "I suspect that, if the patient has met up with no object in his
> infancy on whom he can place some, however little, love and
> trust, he will not come to us in analysis. He will pursue a
> psychotic path alone"
>
> Betty Joseph, 1985, p. 452

P
erhaps the very fact that a person gets in touch with a
clinical service indicates that he is at least minimally
hopeful that someone may be able to help him.* However,
this is only a start; a prospective patient needs to have a modicum
of "love and trust" in an early object relationship as a basic re-
quirement for any creative therapeutic endeavour. Keeping this
tenet in mind, the assessment consultation can begin.

In today's climate, with the proliferation of so many varieties
of therapy, the field of assessment is coming to the fore and being

---

*For the sake of simplicity, throughout the text we use the feminine
gender for the therapist and the masculine gender for the patient, unless
otherwise stated or the usage is obvious.

recognized as increasingly important, and the need for under-standing the parameters of assessment is crucial. Even most of the rigorous analytic trainings do not include assessment as part of their basic curriculum, and many therapists are eager to learn about it. Practitioners, at an early stage in their careers, frequently find themselves in a position of having to do an assessment, pos-sibly with not enough experience. With our long experience as assessors, we would like to open up the discussion on this subject and focus on the main issues, both for educating potential referrers and for helping psychoanalytic psychotherapists develop the necessary skills in assessing.

It is essential to be clear about what we can and cannot offer as psychoanalytic psychotherapists in private practice. In the assess-ment session, we try to pick up all the cues the patient gives us—verbal, non-verbal, visual—in order to predict whether we think he can engage in the therapeutic process creatively.

Although it has frequently been said that the scope of psycho-analysis has broadened to include a much wider range of disturbance, and it is not unusual to assess narcissistic or border-line patients and refer them on for psychotherapy, the basic aim has always remained the same: "To help people who suffer from states of mind that are a source of distress or that have resulted in distressing symptoms" (Laufer & Laufer, 1996). Something that assessors need to bear in mind with patients with a very damaged early history is their propensity to form a strong, immediate at-tachment to the assessor. This can lead to feelings of rejection and abandonment at being passed on to another therapist, which in extreme cases can be insurmountable.

An assessment is not just a matter of taking a social and devel-opmental history; we must also gain access to the patient's inner world to help us consider whether he can use psychoanalytic psy-chotherapy. However, it is not a miniature analysis, which would, "either overwhelm the patient or attach him too much to his [i.e. the analyst's] person at the expense of the smooth evolution of the transference to his eventual analyst" (Klauber, 1971, p. 143). In order to try to understand a patient, an assessment consultation will combine a classical approach with some degree of structure. The somewhat extreme style of the formal, silent analyst—the "fridge-freezer" stance, as one patient described it—is not helpful. On the other hand, if the assessor is too responsive, the boundaries may be blurred, the patient will get a social or emotional response where many of his perceived needs will be gratified, and he will not get a sense of the professional, analysing stance necessary for psychotherapy. As Klauber (1971) comments, in an assessment consultation the patient needs to be put at ease in order to create an environment in which he will be able to tell his life story. It is essential that the initial interview should be therapeutic and not traumatic (Klauber, 1972).

It is often said that if you ask questions, you will only get answers. To enable the patient to reveal more vulnerable parts of himself, his inner life and fantasies, as well as his external reality, the assessor must provide both focus and psychic space for the slow unfolding of material.

The assessment session provides a space that can be therapeutic in itself. The patient can experience a different way of being heard, and the act of putting feelings and experiences into words can give him an entirely different perspective. It is important that a patient comes of his own volition rather than due to pressure from family, partner, friends, or colleagues. This pressure extends into the question of payment for the therapy; there can be a polluting influence, which may lead to an unconscious collusion between the therapist and, for example, a parent who is paying the fees for an adult patient.

Perhaps another question we need to ask ourselves at the assessment consultation is, whom do I represent for the patient? This may be his first experience of a therapeutic relationship, and it will give us some insight into his inner world of object relations if we can understand whether we are predominantly a benign or a hostile object for him. From this very first consultation, we must be aware that our countertransference reflects the patient's transference.

Having gathered a great deal of information from the patient, the assessor will examine it from various psychoanalytic standpoints. Perhaps originally, patients would have been seen in terms of their libidinal development (oral, anal, genital), and one of Freud's criteria for psychological health was based on a person's capacity to work and love. Today, we are likely to include further criteria. For instance, what is the level of ego functioning of the patient, including the predominant defences used? From an object relations point of view, has the patient reached the oedipal triad or is he still functioning in the dyadic mode? And, has he reached the depressive position? Moreover, it is essential to look at what has been called the patient's psychological-mindedness, which involves an acceptance of the unconscious and an ability to use the transference. In addition, however damaged or infantile someone may be, we look to see if he can also take responsibility for himself in an adult way. It also seems to us imperative to look at the current social situation of a patient, as it is not easy to have in therapy a seriously damaged patient who has no network of support in his external life.

If psychoanalytic psychotherapy seems indicated, we must try to explain the process and what will be required of the patient. We must tell him about free association, how important dreams can be, and the reason for using the couch. We say that sessions are fifty minutes long, are at completely regular intervals, and that he is held responsible for paying for missed sessions. He is also told that his therapist will take breaks when there will be no sessions. Thus we try to establish some boundaries and limits to the containment that the therapy can provide.

"The quest for accurate prediction in such a complicated area has within it a considerable degree of omnipotent fantasy" (Garelick, 1994, p. 113). Throughout an assessment session, we need to bear in mind both the opportunities and limitations of psychoanalytic psychotherapy. This is not the treatment of choice for everybody. Furthermore, even if the assessor feels that it is recommended, he must always allow the patient the freedom of options: "Offering patients no choice makes for fear, flight, or submissiveness, but not for an open-minded approach to therapy" (Klauber, 1972).

Our referral, on a pragmatic level, may be dependent on geography, frequency, times, money. Because we make a referral to a specific therapist and it is not our practice to give a list of names, ideally we like to have some idea of an appropriate "match" between patients and therapists. For example, we might not refer a

severely depressed patient to a depressed colleague. Some therapists feel comfortable working with a borderline patient, whereas
others do not. Age and gender of the therapist may be important—middle-aged patients frequently ask for an older therapist:
"I don't want someone who does not know what it's like to be
over 50." Patients with a history of abuse may do better with a
same-sex therapist.

Our ultimate task in assessing is to differentiate between
those for whom the psychoanalytic method is not appropriate and
who may benefit from another form of treatment, those who can
make a serious commitment to intensive work in psychoanalytic
psychotherapy, and finally those "who are willing to accept the
long travail of analysis, without guarantees of success" (Stone,
1954, p. 593).

Résumé of contributors' papers

All the chapters in this book are written by members of the
Clinical Service assessment team of the British Association of
Psychotherapists. We have tried to explore the assessment for
psychoanalytic psychotherapy from various perspectives:

> . . . there are two strands in the assessment interview, an
> empathic attempt to grasp the nature of the patient's predica-
> ment, and a more distanced effort to calculate the likelihood
> of therapeutic success. [Holmes, 1995, p. 28]

We start with an overview of the literature, in which Ruth
Berkowitz demonstrates how many analysts have written about
assessment and that, although the field is quite confused, there
seems to be a consensus on certain aspects of it. Ultimately the
assessment experience relies upon both the conscious and unconscious interaction between therapist and patient.

Judith Barnard bridges the two disciplines of medicine and
psychotherapy, showing where general practitioners might be
able to make an appropriate referral for therapy.

Greenson (1992) has made the interesting point that "A reliable diagnosis is often only possible at the end of treatment" (p.

24). Anne Tyndale takes up this controversial question apropos the place of diagnosis in the assessment consultation.

Judy Cooper and Helen Alfillé, looking at a much-discussed issue that has barely been addressed in the literature, bring into focus the pros and cons of referring patients for once-weekly or more intensive psychoanalytic psychotherapy.

The next two chapters look in some depth at the actual assessment consultation. Arna Davis takes us through the possible communications conveyed by the opening story, both their diversity and depth. Aslan Mordecai and Danuta Waydenfeld illustrate the importance of the parameters of this first setting that the patient encounters, which is the blueprint for any future experience in psychotherapy.

The patient's responses and attachment to the assessor, both positive and negative, will form the basis for the future psychotherapeutic work. Just as an assessment patient may feel he would like to continue with the assessor as his therapist, so we sometimes feel an immediate rapport with a patient. This shows how essential it is to be aware of both transference and countertransference issues in the assessment. Mary Rosalind Stumpfl enables us to see something of how this functions in the consulting-room.

The patient coming for an assessment should be met by a therapist who is clear about the frame—the boundaries regarding the setting and his own person. Philip Hewitt examines the boundaries and potential difficulties that can arise around apparently straightforward interactions and the importance of attending to the non-verbal, almost instinctual, exchanges such as body language and the use of the therapeutic space.

Mira Malovic-Yeeles outlines the difficulties facing the assessor in deciding whether psychotherapy is the treatment of choice and the dangers inherent in referring someone for whom psychotherapy might be harmful.

CHAPTER ONE

Assessment for psychoanalytic psychotherapy: an overview of the literature

Ruth Berkowitz

"I must however make it clear that what I am asserting is that this technique is the only one suited to my individuality; I do not venture to deny that a physician quite differently constituted might find himself driven to adopt a different attitude to his patients and to the task before him"

Freud, 1912e, p. 111

The idea that those seeking psychoanalytic treatment need to be carefully selected by analysts was first proposed by Freud (1904a, 1905a, 1912e, 1937c). On the basis of a meeting, variably called an assessment, a consultation, or an evaluation, the analyst makes an assessment of the prospective patient. If the patient is considered suitable for psychoanalytic psychotherapy, a referral will be made. The number of works cited in this chapter is testimony to the thought and effort that this idea has generated.

While this chapter includes most of the main papers in the field, it does not claim to cover all the material on the subject. Few of the papers are recent—only four of those most quoted having been published in the 1990s—and while it is not obvious why this is so, one could speculate that the whole area of assessment rather than becoming clearer has, in some way, become more blurred. It is, however, a field that has grown somewhat haphazardly: authors have written papers in which terms have been loosely used, in which their ideas have not been related to those of others, and in which questions that seem very fundamental are not raised. Throughout what is now nearly a century of work and thought, a virtual morass of work has burgeoned, punctuated at intervals by review articles that seem to attempt to bring attention at least, and a little order at best, to some of the confusions and loopholes.

What seems to be an omission in most papers is an explanation of *why* an assessment should be done for a treatment such as psychoanalysis. Of course, in the case of selection of patients for supervised analyses and of candidates for training, the need for assessment appears more obvious. However, few authors seem to express their views about the consequences of not assessing patients in this way, although it would seem that there are tacit understandings. Stone (1954) was quite unusual in saying that analysis should not be undertaken in cases where the prognosis looks bad or the personality cannot tolerate it. Similarly, Zetzel (1968), in describing patients whom she considered unsuitable, says that the risk inherent in such patients entering psychoanalytic therapy is a passive dependent transference and serious problems in the terminal phase.

Another omission in most papers is any definition of the process called psychoanalysis; again, for the most part there is tacit agreement about what is meant. It is a serious omission since the rationale for assessment must hinge on the nature of this treatment, and on the demands and rigours of the experience. No single definition seems adequate, but it may be important to recognize that developments in the theory and practice of psychoanalysis have interacted with thinking on assessment.

However, the purpose of this review is

1. To give some account of the work that has been done in the field of what will be called "assessment" in this chapter, with, once again, the unspoken recognition that this is a predictive task. To

put it crudely, what are the aspects that need to be thought about in order that both the patient and the analyst can engage in this process called psychoanalysis or psychoanalytic psychotherapy? The main aspects described here are the qualities of the patient, the personality of the analyst, and the patient—analyst match. This account has a historical perspective in that an attempt is made to look at various aspects of assessment and how these have evolved over time.

2. To describe various aspects of the *process* of assessment. Very few authors define this process, but Pollock's definition (1960) that the purpose is "patient evaluation and suggestions for further procedures" is one that covers the assessment process to be discussed here.

The papers in this review are clinical and research studies, and both of these areas have their strengths and weaknesses. Some of the papers deal with referral to qualified analysts and some with referral to candidates training in psychoanalysis—that is, supervised analyses. One of the limitations of this overview is that constraints of space prevent the comparing and contrasting of these various aspects. Having taken into account this limitation, it is worth noting the comment of Bloch (1979) as regards the research:

> The immense volume of research in the area of assessment has yielded little of practical value and the impact of research on clinical work has been minimal. [p. 205]

As regards supervised analyses, these papers could perhaps be considered comparable to the others on assessment in many ways. One very obvious difference is the context for which the assessment is made. This very general point will be addressed at the end of the chapter in terms of the factors that impinge on the course of an analysis.

For the purposes of this chapter in relation to the treatment that is being considered, Hinshelwood's (1995) approach is followed: in making assessments, his view applies to psychoanalysis as well as to an intensive psychotherapy based on the psychoanalytic method. The terms psychoanalysis and psychoanalytic therapy are used interchangeably.

Patient qualities

The early search for the criteria
defining the psychoanalytic patient

The early descriptions of patient qualities provide evidence of a state of confusion that still continues to be the case. As Baker (1980) said, "In scanning the psychoanalytic literature it is possible to reach the conclusion that psychoanalysis is suitable for everything and nothing " (p. 355). (For excellent reviews of the earlier literature, the reader is referred to Tyson & Sandler, 1971, and Erle & Goldberg, 1979.) From the earliest times, Freud (1904a, 1905a, 1912e, 1937c), outlining his views of the symptoms, qualifications, indications, and contraindications of the prospective psychoanalytic patient, considered it important to look beyond the diagnosis or illness to the whole personality. Chronic cases of psychoneuroses without very violent or dangerous symptoms were considered the most favourable for psychoanalysis. He excluded psychoses, states of confusion, and deeply rooted depression, although at that time he held the view that, by suitable changes in the method, this contraindication could be overcome and that there could be a psychotherapy of the psychoses. In looking beyond the patient's illness to the whole personality, he emphasized intelligence, ethical development (i.e. persons of a reliable character), and those under 50. Over the age of 50, the mass of psychical material, according to him, was no longer manageable, the time required for recovery being too long and the ability to undo the psychical processes beginning to grow weaker. In addition, patients should come to treatment because of their own suffering, not because of the authority of a relative. Tyson and Sandler (1971) quote the work of Jones (1920), who lists certain diagnoses for patient selection such as hysteria, anxiety hysteria, obsessional neurosis, hypochondria, fixation hysteria, and certain psychosomatic disorders such as hay-fever. The character disorders were excluded at this stage, and, as Tyson and Sandler point out, it was only when Reich published his book (1953) that this diagnostic group appeared on lists.

Authors such as Fenichel (1945) and Glover (1954b), while offering lists of diagnoses, added their views on the important characteristics of the personality behind the diagnosis that should be considered, and they furthered the idea that the qualities of the person behind the illness were important and that diagnosis alone was an inadequate guide to patient selection.

Fenichel (1945) included hysteria, compulsions and pregenital conversions, stuttering and psychogenic tics, neurotic depressions, character disturbances, perversions, addictions and impulse neuroses, and psychoses, including manic-depressive psychosis and schizophrenia. This notion that the diagnosis is linked to the person was also emphasized by Glover (1954b), who took into account personality, life style, and the developmental stage of early life in which the illness could be seen as primarily rooted. He based his diagnoses on a developmental approach—for example, anxiety hysteria having its origins between 4 and 5 years of age, obsessional neurosis between 3 and 4, and psychoses in the first three years of life. Glover assigned his list of diagnoses to three categories: accessible, moderately accessible, and slightly accessible. In the "accessible" category, he included such diagnoses as anxiety hysteria, conversion hysteria, and mixed neuroses, but the deciding feature was that the predominant anxiety arises from the later infantile genital phases of development. Included amongst other diagnoses in the "moderately accessible" category was the average organized obsessional neurosis and obsessional character, and some sexual perversions, having their roots mainly in pregenital layers of development. Those diagnoses linked most closely with psychotic structures and psychoses were included in the "slightly accessible" category, of which he says endogenous depression is the most favourable and the pure paranoias the least. The use of the term "accessible" (although not new, as it was used by Freud) added a further dimension to the issue of assessment. Glover's use of the term was linked to the transference: the earlier the fixation points, the more tenuous is the positive transference bond and the less accessible is the patient to the opening-up process. Accessibility has been elaborated as a concept by others, in particular, Tyson and Sandler (1971), who in their paper suggest that it appears to be related to the factors that go into the making of a treatment alliance. This is discussed in greater detail in later sections.

While some authors were concerned with diagnosis as being too limiting, others such as Stone (1954) were concerned that the method screened out those who might otherwise be selected for psychoanalytic therapy. He did describe certain conditions that he considered to have the "least part" in psychoanalysis. Firstly, there were psychoses, addictions, and perversions, which were considered problematic because they compete with the therapy in terms of providing relief from painful tension. Secondly, there were those psychosomatic problems that may be indicative of the severity of psychoses. However, in his paper "The Widening Scope of Indications for Psychoanalysis" (1954), he made a plea for the classical technique in some instances to be modified to accommodate certain patients:

> My own clinical experience and observation lead me to be-lieve that *too* great approximation to the mathematical ideal in certain references is antitherapeutic. [p. 574]

He goes on to say that there may, in some instances, be a need for deviation because it may be impossible for some patients to work with total emotional detachment. However, the deviation should not be too great and should be seen as a technique, not as a personal gratification or as a panicky fear of rule breaking. Stone's paper can be understood mainly in terms of widening the scope of psychoanalysis—that is, being somewhat more flexible in method—to include those patients who formerly might not have been taken into treatment.

> However, psychoanalysis may legitimately be invoked and indeed *should* be invoked for many very ill people, of good personality resources, who are probably inaccessible to cure by other methods, who are willing to accept the long travail of analysis without guarantees of success. [pp. 593–594]

There is also the sense in which he widened the scope to thoughts about not only the analytic method but the role of the analyst in the analytic task. This is discussed in later sections. The idea that diagnosis on its own can be misleading was one highlighted in a paper by Zetzel (1968), "The So-called Good Hysteric", in which she described four categories of patients who had been diagnosed as hysteric. These patients were differentiated from one another on a variety of criteria—developmental, their defences, their work and academic achievements, their birth order in family of origin. Most interestingly, she marked out those whom she termed the "so-called good hysteric" in terms of the following criteria: absence or significant separation from parents in the first four years of life; serious pathology in one or more parents, often associated with a broken or unhappy marriage; serious and prolonged physical illness in childhood; a continuing hostile dependent relationship with the mother, who is seen as devaluing and rejecting or is devalued; and, finally, an absence of meaningful and sustained object relations with either sex. She was perhaps one of the first to consider the role of the patient's object relations—not only the early, but also the current object relations—as being important.

The early work mainly addressed the issues of diagnosis but also, more generally, patient qualities behind the diagnosis. Terms were, however, not defined, the purpose of assessments was unclear, and by 1971 the field had become complex if not confusing. The paper by Tyson and Sandler in that year addressed both these issues. They wisely entitled their paper "Problems in the Selection of Patients for Psychoanalysis", thereby avoiding the very pitfalls into which others had fallen: namely, using in a loose way such terms as indications/contraindications, suitability, accessibility, and analysability. "Indications", they suggested, were "signs and symptoms", whereas suitability was more to do with the qualities and capacities of the patient. Assessment for treatment, according to them, depends more on criteria of suitability than on indications. They suggest that instead of talking about the suitability of the patient for the treatment, it is more appropriate to talk about the suitability of the treatment for the person. Perhaps there is greater hope for the individual if suitability is understood in this way, with there being possibilities of other treatments that may offer something of more value to this person. The notion of accessibility, referred to earlier, was also used by Freud (1905a) in terms of whether analysis could reach and influence the patient. This is understood in terms of what has come to be known as "psychological-mindedness"—the capacity to think in psychological terms, to see connections between events and feelings in himself. Tyson and Sandler (1971) understand accessibility in terms of the

> various components necessary for an adequate treatment
> alliance i.e. the capacity to tolerate a certain amount of frus-

tration, the capacity to regard oneself as one might regard another, a degree of basic trust, identification with the aims of treatment etc. [p. 217]

In addressing the issue of accessibility, the area of assessment is broadened, from the diagnosis and the person behind it, to the patient in the context of a psychoanalytic treatment.

Tyson and Sandler also discuss the term "analysability" frequently used in papers, a term that they regard as having disadvantages because it obscures the distinction between whether the analyst understands the patient and whether the patient can benefit from the analytic procedure at any time. It also perhaps introduces the thorny problem of the aims of psychoanalysis and the issue of how one might judge the success or otherwise of an assessment, let alone an analysis.

Tyson and Sandler's paper, then, very usefully reviews the literature up to 1971, taking as their framework Freud's criteria of suitability:

1. The upper age limit set at 50 by Freud was increased by subsequent writers, notably Abraham (1919), who suggested that the age of the neurosis was more important than the age of the patient. Tyson and Sandler themselves conclude that "an assessment must take into account the changes due to age in the individual patient rather than the simple factor of age itself" (p. 220).

2. Intelligence or education, it is suggested by Tyson and Sandler, should be considered more in terms of whether or not the patient can develop a treatment alliance and a sufficient degree of insight.

3. As regards moral and ethical considerations, Tyson and Sandler, while quoting authors such as Jones (1920) and Bibring (1937), suggest (as apparently did Fenichel, 1945) that a patient with one type of moral problem may be acceptable to one analyst and not to another. In such a case, they indicate that the analyst should not try to set aside feelings but, rather, should refer the patient elsewhere.

4. Freud (1905a) had suggested that the patient should be motivated by the fact that he suffers from his symptoms but then

later (1926d [1925]) identified secondary gain—that is, drawing as much advantage from the symptoms as possible. Tyson and Sandler warn that some patients may have so much to lose in the form of secondary gain that analysis may not be a viable proposition.

Tyson and Sandler's paper brings together the early thinking and usefully makes distinctions between formerly undefined terms, as well as reviewing the literature in the way outlined above. Their paper also draws attention to the complexity of the assessment process, indicating that any recommendations for psychoanalytic treatment need to take into account the qualities of the patient but also the possible treatment alliance and the patient–analyst match. In spite of the growing awareness of the complexity of the assessment task, the search continued for those patient qualities that would identify the ideal patient for psychoanalysis. Tyson and Sandler comment that the so-called criteria of suitability represent ideal conditions and that "It would seem that we may be in the paradoxical position of finding that the patient who is ideally suited for analysis, is in no need of it!" (p. 227).

The continuing search for patient qualities

Considerable work, both clinical and research, has gone into the search for patient qualities, and Waldhorn's (1960) dictum "sick enough to need it and healthy enough to stand it" encompasses both the notion of the diagnosis as much as the person behind it. In a similar vein, Greenson (1967) suggests that a diagnosis may not tell us much about the healthy resources of the patient and that even perversions and borderline diagnoses have "varying degrees of healthy resources. Yet it is their supply of assets, not the pathology which may be the decisive factor" (p. 53). He goes on to suggest that what needs to be assessed is the patient's endowment in regard to the specific demands of psychoanalytic therapy, which is a time-consuming, long-range, and costly therapy and by its nature is very frequently painful. The search has, therefore, continued for the qualities that reflect both the pathological and the healthy aspects of the patient. (It is perhaps worth noting that

Bachrach & Leaff, 1978, in their review of the literature, listed 390 individual but widely overlapping items that different authors thought important in predicting analysability.)

CATEGORIES OF PATIENT QUALITIES

It is important to note in the work that is described below on the categorization of patient qualities that a variety of methods of assessment were used. These have been described by Bachrach and Leaff (1978) as follows:

1. clinical interview, with emphasis on life history—in recent times emphasis has been placed more on the experience within the interview itself;

2. diagnostic psychological testing (Kernberg et al., 1972);

3. meeting of a committee to make decisions, which is used mainly in supervised cases for training;

4. assessment based on the outcome of the treatment.

Not only are there these variations in *methods* of assessment (which has been touched on above), but variations in the *purpose* of assessment. Limentani (1972) considered assessment from three different points of view—of private patients, of supervised cases, and of candidates for training—and indicated that there needs to be a clearer definition of the purpose of assessment in these terms.

Bachrach and Leaff (1978), in their extensive review of the literature, described qualities of the patients in terms of the categories outlined below, which are used here as a framework. Examples are given, but because of limited space these are not exhaustive but are aimed at giving some sense of the thinking and its evolution over time.

• *Adequacy of general personality functioning: including all references to adequacy of adaptive functioning, severity of illness, severity of symptoms, diagnosis, ego strength, reality testing, sublimatory potentials, adaptive regression, defence, thinking, intellectual abilities, and capacity for verbalization*

1. *Diagnosis, severity of symptoms.* Some of the thinking in this area has been discussed above, but there are subsequent views that are worth noting. Greenson (1967) suggested that psychoanalysis was contraindicated for the various forms of schizophrenia and manic-depressive psychosis, but the case was questionable for such disorders as impulse neuroses, perversions, addictions, delinquencies, and borderline cases. Klauber (1971) expressed wariness about patients with psychosomatic complaints without other conflicts, and those with hypochondriasis. More recently, Coltart (1987) has pointed out that the term character disorder has been elaborated and that there have been advances in the theory and treatment of severe narcissistic disorders. She expresses, however, some reservations about depression with a kind of affective flatness and projective mechanisms, which should make one consider a concealed narcissistic disorder, as well as about a tentative diagnosis of the false self. However, she says that other situations formerly regarded as not suitable for selection for psychoanalysis—for example, psychosomatic states, delinquency, psychotic signs or behaviour trends, too-long periods of previous treatment, very high levels of anxiety and tension, patient older than the therapist—may all be dealt with by psychoanalytic therapists who have an interest in, and extended knowledge of, a particular area of disturbance. The implication is that psychoanalysis may be a treatment of choice for a far greater range of patients than formerly thought. Garelick (1994) notes a trend away from diagnosis to the nature of the relationship and transactions between patient and assessor.

2. *Psychological-mindedness.* This has been described in various ways by different authors: a capacity for self-observation or self-appraisal as opposed to rationalization (Stone, 1954); an ability to take a distance from his own emotional experience (Namnum, 1968): the ability to carry out ego functions that are in contradiction to one another, such as in free association, and to regress in thinking but also rebound from regression in his relationship to the analyst; the ability to have resilient and flexible ego functions (Greenson, 1967); the ability to think in psychological terms; and, finally, the ability to see connections between events and feelings

in himself (Tyson & Sandler, 1971). Sashin, Eldred, and Van Amerongen (1975), in an attempt to rate the usefulness of specific factors in the reports of individual evaluation interviews on patients accepted for supervised psychoanalytic treatment, found that there was very little inter-rater reliability on the criterion of psychological-mindedness. From clinical interviews, however, Coltart (1987) expressed the view that if the patient shows a lively curiosity and a genuine concern about internal reality and

> if he can make a tenuous link between the idea of relief from psychic pain and an increase in self knowledge, and then shows some real pleasure in finding out some tiny thing about himself in the initial interview, this is one of the best criteria for the analytical approach. [p. 23]

3. *Ego strength.* According to Kernberg (Kernberg et al., 1972), good initial ego strength is correlated with degree of improvement. Sashin et al. (1975), in the study mentioned above, found low inter-rater reliability on this criterion of ego strength. Baker (1980), in a paper on suitability for supervised cases for training, approached the question of ego strength from the perspective of primitive defences, suggesting that their widespread presence is an ominous sign, the more so sometimes when they appear to be in the service of ego stability. He goes on to say that the successful operation of such defences can mask the ominous signs of ego weakness, such as the capacity to tolerate anxiety and the precarious mastery of impulse control.

- *Object relations: including all references to object-relatedness, narcissism, tolerance for separation, object constancy, and capacity for transference and working alliance*

Object relations have been viewed mainly in terms of the earliest relationships, although some authors such as Zetzel (1968) and Sashin et al. (1975) drew attention to the current relationships of the patient as well. More recently, the patient's reaction to the assessment process—their response to the assessor, the transference, and countertransference—have become increasingly important.

1. *Early object relationships.* This was emphasized by Stone (1954), who took a longitudinal history and considered the character and pattern of relationships with people. Aarons (1962) suggested that a high initial quality of interpersonal relationships—that is, the person's earliest object relationship—may provide a reliable basis for an assessment of his analysability. Object constancy and the capacity for differentiation of self and object representation was emphasized by Huxster, Lower, and Escott (1975). Others (Knapp, Levin, McCarter, Wetment, & Zetzel, 1960; Zetzel, 1965; Namnum, 1968) have all noted the importance of the capacity for object relations. Sashin et al. (1975) noted that those who left their analysis prematurely (within six months or even after three years) had a poor relationship with the same-sex parent. However, Kantrowitz et al. (1989) in contrast suggests, on the basis of a research pilot study, that the level and quality of object relationships is not predictive of outcome.

2. *Object relations within the assessment setting.* Stone (1954) suggests that the patient's reaction to the examiner is of importance and should be noted. This aspect has been given more attention recently. Klauber (1971) suggests that it is primarily the quality of the rapport formed as a result of glimpsing the emotional and intellectual process that will enable the patient and the consultant to judge whether the patient can make further use of the experience. In his view, the assessment is

> based on a complex assessment of defences and motives and arrives at a richer and profoundly relevant picture of the personality extending far back into the history of the patient. The most important thing is for it to take account of the intensity of the compulsions to repeat old patterns of behaviour, both within and outside the analysis. [pp. 150–151]

Hinshelwood (1995) considers, in addition to infantile object relationships and the current life situation, that it is essential to take into account the relationship to the assessor. Ogden (1989) sees the patient's history as being conveyed unconsciously in the form of transference–countertransference experience. This, he says, is the patient's living past, the set of object relations established in infancy and early childhood which has come to constitute the structure of the patient's mind both as the content and context of his psychological life.

• *Motivation*

Although motivation has been regarded as an important variable in selection of patients by some (Aarons, 1962; Greenson, 1967; Knapp et al., 1960; Sashin et al., 1975; Tyson & Sandler, 1971), Kernberg (Kernberg et al., 1972) did not regard it as playing an important role. Similarly, Kantrowitz (1987) said that not only was it difficult to evaluate but it was also not predictive of outcome.

• *Affect organization, including references to availability of and toler-ance for anxiety, frustration, and depression*

Authors have referred to this area in a variety of ways. Stone (1954) emphasized a capacity for patience and deliberate tolerance of unavoidable suffering. Zetzel (1965) wrote of the capacity to withstand anxiety and depression, Kernberg (Kernberg et al., 1972) of a high initial anxiety tolerance, and Tyson and Sandler (1971) of a capacity to tolerate and recognize affect. Once again, Kantrowitz et al. (1989) suggest that affect availability and toler-ance are not predictive of successful outcome.

• *Character qualities*

This has been described in different ways by various authors: the need for a high degree of honesty and integrity (Greenson, 1967); the need to be reliable in the first place (Klauber, 1971); the need to have moral awareness and integrity (Coltart, 1987).

• *Superego factors*

This would include factors to do with a harsh superego, need for punishment, self-deprecation, and a history of reactions of unwor-thiness to successful achievements, which obviously would be regarded as less favourable when considering assessment. This was described in terms of deprecation and self-castigation (Stone, 1954), low self-esteem (Zetzel, 1965), or basic deficit in self-esteem (Huxster et al., 1975).

• *Demographic factors*

Age has been discussed above. Other factors such as occupation and life situation were considered relevant by Stone (1954). However, Bloch (1979) suggested that age, sex, marital status, educational achievement, and socioeconomic status were not of prognostic relevance. Huxster et al. (1975) noted that achievements in school and work were important, as did Coltart (1987) who suggested that the person who fails at everything will fail at analysis as well.

• *External factors*

Greenson (1967) suggested that prospective patients should not be in the midst of a life crisis. According to Klauber (1971), it is advisable to be wary of those who are making their own or someone else's life impossible. Bachrach and Leaff (1978) listed the following qualities:

> Taken together these studies suggest that persons most suitable for classical psychoanalysis are those whose functioning is generally adequate; they have good ego strength, effective reality testing and sublimatory channels, and are able to cope flexibly, communicate verbally, think in secondary-process terms, and regress in the service of the ego with sufficient intellect to negotiate the tasks of psychoanalysis; their symptoms are not predominantly severe, and their diagnoses fall within a "neurotic" spectrum. Such persons are able to form a transference neurosis and therapeutic alliance, are relatively free of narcissistic pathology, have good object relations with friends, parents, and spouses, and have been able to tolerate early separations and deprivations without impairment of object constancy; they are, therefore, able to experience genuine triangular conflict. They are motivated for self-understanding, change, and to relieve personal suffering. They are persons with good tolerance for anxiety, depression, frustration, and suffering and are able to experience surges of feeling without loss of impulse control or disruption of secondary process mooring of thought. Their character attitudes and traits are well-suited to the psychoanalytic work, i.e. psychological mindedness. Superego is integrated and tolerant. They are

mainly in their late twenties or early thirties and have not experienced past psychotherapeutic failure or difficulties. Of all these qualities, those relating to ego strength and object relations are most important. [pp. 885–886]

The above quotation gives what could be thought of as the definitive catalogue of characteristics of the ideal patient, but as early as 1960 Knapp et al. said the following after describing their study of a review of 100 supervised cases:

> Certainly our work suggests the impossibility of treating patients as an aggregate of unrelated and separate qualities and the difficulty, not to say impossibility, of carrying out most studies of this kind by evaluation of patients alone. The attributes and experience of the analyst, the establishment of the analytic situation, and finally, the development and resolution of the transference neurosis must all be taken into consideration. [p. 476]

Perhaps most telling of all is the comment by Bachrach and Leaff (1978)—which is still applicable—that the majority of studies fail to indicate the evidence for their conclusions, the data upon which they are based, the populations referred to, selection biases, and, in general, the extent to which one investigation may truly replicate another. Very few studies specify what is meant by psychoanalysis; furthermore, as the work of Kantrowitz et al. (1989) indicates, it is questionable whether there is good agreement about the meaning of terms used. It would appear from the papers described here that there is far from total agreement; in particular, the work of Kantrowitz et al. (1989) questions some of the clinical findings. It is probably still true to say, as Bachrach and Leaff (1978) suggest, that the quantitative findings are superficial and those that are clinical are limited from a methodological point of view.

However, at the end of their very comprehensive and lengthy review Bachrach and Leaff (1978) do conclude that the studies of all kinds, despite their limitations, indicate a considerable degree of agreement about the qualities deemed to make a person a suitable candidate for psychoanalysis: the better the pre-treatment level of personality organization, the more favourable the prospect.

Bearing all this in mind, and the tremendous amount of work and effort that has gone into the establishment of those patient qualities that would make a person a suitable candidate for psychoanalysis, it would seem that, as Garelick (1994) suggests, there has been movement away from diagnosis and that the search for individual factors has been unfruitful. The growing trend is towards the nature of the relationship and transactions between patient and assessor. Reservations about the emphasis only on the patient's qualities have been growing, and there is an increasing awareness of the importance of the role of the analyst and the analytic fit in the outcome of the analysis. Since the qualities of the analyst and that of the analytic match are even more difficult to assess than the patient qualities, much less attention has been devoted to them.

The personality of the analyst and the patient–analyst match

The personality of the analyst

Freud (1905a) himself acknowledged the role of the analyst's personality in the analysis:

> It is not a modern dictum but an old saying of physicians that these diseases are not cured by the drug but by the physician, that is, by the personality of the physician, inasmuch as through it he exerts a mental influence. [p. 259]

As early as 1938, Clara Thompson wrote a paper entitled "Notes on the Psychoanalytic Significance of the Choice of Analyst", saying

> that pertaining to the analyst's part in the collaboration is the more glaringly inadequate. One seldom finds an account of anything that suggests the differences in personality of various psychoanalysts or the significant entering of the analyst's personality in the whole protracted process. Many analysts, however, must have failed with some patient who did better elsewhere; must have carried to completion some patient who had failed with a preceding analyst. If one knew practical psychoanalytic experience only from the papers printed, one might be tempted to assume that the analyst as a personality in reality does not exist, that he never says anything, that he

never leaves the impress of his opinion on the patient in any way, that he never makes any mistakes, that in short, he is not human but a fountain of completely detached wisdom in no way affected personally by anything which goes on. [p. 205]

This question of the personality of the analyst was considered by Stone (1954), who in his discussion of the analyst himself suggested that the analyst needs to know his own capacities (intellectual and emotional), special predilections, interests, and emotional textures, since "he may profoundly influence prognosis, and thus—in a tangible way—the indications" (p. 592). In the same journal issue, Anna Freud (1954) wrote what she considered were "technically subversive thoughts" (p. 619):

> But—and this seems important to me—so far as the patient has a healthy part of his personality, his real relationship to the analyst is never wholly submerged. With due respect for the necessary strictest handling and interpretation of the transference, I still feel that we should leave room somewhere for the realization that analyst and patient are also two real people, of equal adult status, in a real personal relationship to each other. I wonder whether our—at times complete— neglect of this side of the matter is not responsible for some of the hostile reactions which we get from our patients and which we are apt to ascribe to "true transference" only. [pp. 618–619]

Frank (1956), in writing about what he described as the "standard technique", made the point that in his opinion psychoanalysis is a "subjective, solipsistic science, and I do not think we can shun our personalities in discussing technical matters" (p. 282). In a similar way, as mentioned before, Knapp et al. (1960) emphasized the importance of recognizing the attributes and experience of the analyst.

In 1968, Waldhorn, writing on the "lessons from the second analysis" suggested that, in those cases which by all reasonable evaluations appear suitable for analysis but prove to be incompletely or unsatisfactorily analysed,

> the analyst's technical and theoretical limitations are implicated in most instances. Failure to understand the dynamics

of the patient's problems or confusion about the course and sequence of the development of the analysis predispose to anxiety and errors in technique of many sorts. [p. 360]

This comment needs to be seen against one of the issues considered to be a contraindication for analysis, and that is lengthy previous analysis. Is there a prejudice against those patients for whom analysis has been unsatisfactory, a closing of ranks against an "unsuitable patient" rather than a search for an understanding of that particular analytic situation? Limentani (1972) takes a more rounded view of the situation:

> On the basis of my own experience and that derived from observation of supervised analyses and verbal reports from senior colleagues, I have come to recognize that many unsatisfactory outcomes are often due to a combination of factors arising from both analyst *and* patient. [p. 71]

There is, however, at least one dissident voice in this—that of Kernberg (Kernberg et al., 1972), who holds the view that the skill and personality of the analyst is greatly overridden by patient factors. Kantrowitz et al. (1989) quotes Tartakoff (Panel, 1981), who suggested that it is the personal attributes of the analyst that are crucial in determining what the analyst responds to and communicates in treating a patient.

It would seem, then, that there is concern that an assessment of patient qualities is not sufficient and may be qualified or compromised by the role of the analyst's personality in the analytic experience.

The patient–analyst match

Thompson (1938) suggested that analysts ought to consider their specific liabilities and thereby learn from experience the type of case with whom they do and do not have success, thus saving patients' time and possible discouragement by sending them elsewhere. Pollock (1960), in his paper on the role and responsibilities of the analytic consultant, regarded it as an accepted fact that familiarity with a particular cultural background will permit the analyst to appreciate certain value systems, customs, and attitudes: "Without such appreciations by the analyst, things might be misunderstood or thought of as having undue pathological significance" (p. 365). In addition, he says that patients may have strong views about the attributes of the analyst which may be defensive but, if regarded only in this way and not respected, may lead to an unsuitable match between analyst and patient, and the analysis may therefore fail.

In the paper by Waldhorn (1968) and the response to it by Liberman (1968), the match between patient and prospective analyst is regarded as a crucial factor. Liberman, taking up the issue of fit or match, offers a suggestion that more information on the question of fit could come from unpublished qualifying papers and points out from his own supervisory experience how differently a patient may react depending on the way he is focused by the analyst (p. 363). Shapiro (quoted by Kantrowitz et al., 1989) cites the fit between the analyst and patient as the most important element in the training analysis unless the initial pathology is too severe for steady progress to occur.

The neglect of this area and the relative paucity of information is pointed out by Bachrach, Weber, and Solomon (1985):

> It is in the area of what transpires in the analytic dyad, i.e. the analytic process, the quality and effectiveness of interventions, the effect of countertransference, and the suitability of the match between analyst and analysand where effective formal methods of investigation are most lacking and most urgently required. [p. 387]

The assessment process

Several aspects of the assessment process are discussed below because, in an overview of this kind, it is relevant to consider developments in approach; more importantly, however, they could be seen as potentially having an impact on the course of the analysis, in combination with the patient and analyst qualities and the match between them:

1. the referral for the assessment;
2. conducting the assessment;
3. one or more meetings;
4. referring on.

The referral for the assessment

The referral for the assessment is not often explicitly considered as a factor in the assessment although it is sometimes alluded to in an oblique way. For example, those patients who are sent by relatives, or indeed sometimes by professionals, and who attend the assessment meeting only because of being sent, are often seen as patients who are unlikely to engage in the analytic process. Freud (1904a) saw it as a contraindication if a patient submitted to seeking treatment because of a relative's authority. Aarons (1962) did not see it in this way, suggesting that the fact that they had come to the assessment was sufficient motivation. In the same year, Pollock wrote a very comprehensive paper entitled "The Role and Responsibilities of the Psychoanalytic Consultant", in which he covered many aspects of the whole assessment process and saw as significant the issue of how the patient gets to the consultant. He emphasized how details of the referral may yield important clues as to the patient's motivation, anxiety level, and resistance patterns, as well as fantasies, expectations, and goals. Along the same lines but nearly thirty years later, Garelick (1994) makes very similar points about the importance of attending to the context of the referral, the nature of the referral pattern, and the system from which the patient has been referred. Hinshelwood (1995) adds another perspective to this issue, suggesting that object relationships in the form of transference and countertransference may often be discerned before the interview in the manner of the referral itself:

> Thus, the referral is often made on the basis of the referrer's unconscious awareness of a specific relationship. It is a kind of "acting out" on the part of the referrer who is caught up unconsciously in one of these object relationships I have been

describing. This is not to the discredit of the referrer, as the awareness of these kinds of relationship is not his field of work and expertise. It is ours. But it is an added clue for us to the patient's core object relationships. [p. 163]

Conducting the assessment

The earlier writers such as Stone (1954), Waldhorn (1960), and Zetzel (1965) tended to take a longitudinal history. Garelick (1994) suggests that one of the important and, perhaps, controversial issues is the activity of the assessor that involves searching out information as opposed to using a technique of free association and the slow unfolding of material. Schubart (1989) and Shapiro (1984) recommend using an associative procedure from the start, evenly suspended attention, and not extracting information. Klauber (1971) and Coltart (1987) seem to adopt an intermediate position giving the patient something of the analytic experience, but at the same time they do not advocate sitting in silence.

Klauber's view is that in the consultation or assessment meeting the role is more an advisory one, directed to the functioning ego of the patient, since such an important decision needs to be made with powers of judgement in operation. Coltart's (1987) view is that

This may involve some questioning, some interpretation, some link making comments, sympathy expressed only in your whole attitude of extremely attentive listening, and some concise summarizing of your own views towards the end of the interview. [p. 26]

Ogden (1989) tries to give the patient a sense of what it means to be in analysis. He does not favour taking a history, since his view is that

a patient's history is not a static entity that is gradually un-earthed; rather, it is an aspect of the patient's conscious and unconscious conception of himself that is in a continual state of evolution and flux. [p. 191]

Garelick (1994) provides a detailed account of his assessment technique, giving the patient an analytic type of experience, taking up issues in the here and now, monitoring the reaction of the patient, and identifying one's own countertransference. He advocates not taking a history initially, although he might do so to relieve anxiety. The history taking would serve to make links revealing the pattern of the patient's interpersonal relationships, separation problems, and a compulsion to repeat. He regards this as potentially educational for the patient, conveying some understanding that the past links up with the present. Hinshelwood's view (1995) is that assessments for psychoanalytic psychotherapy should be no less psychodynamic than psychotherapy itself, and he values making interpretations, even transference interpretations, for two reasons: firstly, the patient's response gives some idea of suitability and psychological-mindedness; secondly, it is a good preparation because it gives a taste of psychotherapy.

One or more meetings

The question of whether there should be a "trial analysis" was a concern in the early days. Freud (1912e) saw the question of trial analysis as sparing the patient the feeling that an attempted cure had failed, but it was also a way of taking a sounding to get to know the case and decide on the suitability for psychoanalysis. It was favoured by Glover (1954b), though not by Greenson (1967): "only the actual experience of a period of analysis can safely determine whether a patient is suitable for psychoanalysis" (p. 55). Tyson and Sandler (1971) point out some disadvantages, such as the patient having started analysis and, therefore, being eager to continue. Trial analyses seem no longer to be an issue, although the question of a single interview as opposed to extended assessments remains a controversial one. Pollock (1960) was opposed to extended interviews, as he said that this interfered with the transference. This particular dialectic between those who advocate extensive interviews and those who think that this interferes with the natural development of the analytic process is one pointed out by Bachrach and Leaff (1978) in their major review. Coltart (1987) appears to conduct single diagnostic interviews, although Garelick (1994) favours extended assessments for the following reasons: the assessor can have a more analytic stance, the patient can have more of an experience of what psychotherapy is going to be like, and the patient is likely to be more involved in the decision-making process. While there is an anxiety expressed by some that a strong transference will develop, Garelick believes that it works towards facilitating a working alliance with the next therapist, and it enables the assessor to metabolize, process, and verbalize primitive communications.

Referring on

If the view were taken that the role of the assessor is only to make an assessment of the patient, then this issue of the referral process should not be included here. If, however, a broader view is taken that any assessment of the patient's problems and qualities for psychoanalytic therapy depends not only on these problems and qualities but on the analyst and the match between patient and analyst, then consideration of the referral process is essential. Thompson (1938) considered the referral important, as did Pollock (1960). He, as mentioned before, considered that value systems should be taken into account, as well as patient preferences, which may have some validity and may not always be resistance. Pollock recommended that reality factors should be considered such as availability, economic range of the patient's resources, and the geographical location. Beyond that, if possible, other considerations are age, sex, marital and parental status, experience, and culture. If there is time, the prospective analyst's temperament and blind spots should be taken into account.

Pollock is aware, as well, that there may be occasions when the relationship between the assessor and the prospective analyst can stir up performance anxieties in the analyst. He also points out that the manner in which the information is given to the prospective analyst is important and should be done in such a way that the future analyst is free of a sense of loyalty and obligation. It is of interest that, at this early stage, such sensitivity can be shown when considering the possible impact of complex variables on the course of an analysis. Tyson and Sandler (1971) quote Fenichel (1945), who suggested that a patient may be suitable for one analyst and not another. They themselves suggest that the analyst himself might feel reluctant, and then it is important to refer the patient elsewhere. Klauber (1971), in pointing out the tremendous responsibility in recommending someone for an analytic treatment, indicates one hazard:

> an underlying conflict of value systems between patient and analyst may cause a permanent discontent which the patient is unable to articulate and which may force him to make painful psychic adjustments that can only gradually be thrown off after the analysis is ended. [p. 142]

Coltart (1987) tries to match the patient with a therapist, being aware of colleagues' capabilities and special talents, believing as she does in the process of matching, since some therapists have gifts for some sorts of patients and others for others.

* * *

The attention to these factors highlights the complexity of the whole process of assessment and that making a judgement at the start of the analytic process to recommend treatment is a risky one, with a whole range of factors impinging on the analysis: the qualities of the patient, of the analyst, of the match between the two, of the process of assessment from before the patient appears at the assessor's door to when he is referred on.

Conclusions

To make a recommendation for psychoanalytic therapy is a serious and at times risky decision. It is serious for the patient, because of the investment of time and money, as well as carrying the potential for difficult and painful experiences. At worst, it can be a damaging experience, considering the effect on the very deprived patient of the frustrations of the analytic setting and/or the effect of the stripping of fragile defences. It is also an investment on the part of the analyst. To conduct an analysis where little progress is made, or which is an experience too difficult to bear, and can become interminable, should also be avoided.

It was said at the beginning of the chapter that an assessment is at some level a predictive exercise. In making such a prediction, it initially seemed wise to base it on those factors that seem most easily assessed, and in the case of psychoanalytic psychotherapy those have been patient qualities. As has been noted, these qualities burgeoned into hundreds, and while the value of this work has been questioned, it has brought to attention the importance of considering not only the diagnosis but, as Freud said, the personality behind the diagnosis. Both the unhealthy and healthy aspects need consideration, and the conclusion that object relations and ego strength are the most important make considerable sense in terms of the analytic task that the patient faces. This involves the capacity to form a transference relationship, and of course such a relationship will have the quality of earlier relationships. Furthermore, the capacity to both experience and reflect on this relies to a large extent on the ego strength of the patient. At the point of assessment, the qualities of the patient are the factors that seem most available as evidence for making the prediction. This, as has been indicated, is far from being the whole story, and the course of the analysis can be affected by the personality of the analyst as well as the match between them. While assessors may try to select and match, there are few satisfactory ways of evaluating these factors except in a post hoc manner. Of course, other factors may impact on the course of the analysis, such as the process of referral. In addition, there have been changes and developments in the assessment process itself, with a greater focus on the object relationship in the here and now, the transference, and the countertransference.

These are, of course, broad generalizations and, as mentioned earlier, are based on both clinical and research papers. Both types of paper present difficulties: clinical papers may struggle with definitions, whereas research papers, in an attempt at rigour and clarity, may filter out the meaning. Some of the papers have addressed the issue of selection for supervised analyses, none of which seem to add much to the question of how the selection of such prospective patients differs fundamentally from other patients, although the paper by Baker (1980) is extremely useful in providing some guidelines for recognizing some very vulnerable patients. Many of the same considerations seem to apply to supervised cases, and the question of "staying power" so that students can complete their training is one that Limentani (1972) considers is overemphasized. There are particular considerations in a training experience that may influence the course of the analysis, such as the nature of the referral and the supervisory experience (Epstein, 1990).

A serious methodological problem in this field relates to the issue of outcome. Some of the papers are based on work in which it has been possible to make some judgements at the end of the analyses, but there are problems in defining what is meant by a completed analysis (Erle & Goldberg, 1979). It was also difficult to distinguish between the development of the analytic process and therapeutic benefit, the latter sometimes occurring without the former (Erle & Goldberg, 1984).

One of the most difficult problems and perhaps most obvious omission is the vagueness and confusion about the definition of psychoanalysis (Erle & Goldberg, 1984). Sometimes the impression is given that this treatment is rather like standard medication taken in the form of tablets, and indeed this was referred to by Frank (1956) as the standard technique. Stone (1954) had tried earlier to address this problem, suggesting that some patients should be selected but that there should be deviations of some kind in the technique to accommodate their needs. Frank (1956) suggested trying to cast the net wider and, by modification of the treatment technique, make it available to patients who otherwise could not be treated by psychological means. He goes on to say:

> I believe that in the group of narcissistic character disorders, particularly if they are deprived, the standard technique is contraindicated. Neither the nursery of children nor the human condition itself, as such, has the psychological climate of the synthetic artificiality of the really nonneutral *but pretending-to-be-so* analyst. I wonder whether the standard technique itself ought not to be *humanized.* [p. 280]

In their review, Bachrach and Leaff (1978) also point out this limitation in the literature and do not give any specific definition of classical analysis because such a definition is not included in most papers. Perhaps this raises the very difficult question that Erle and Goldberg (1979) also raise, as to which modifications of the basic model are consistent with an acceptable concept of analysis. However, as Coltart (1987) points out, there have been advances in technique and in theory—as evidenced by the work of Steiner, Kernberg, Kohut, Symington, and others—on borderline and narcissistic disorders.

While there are limitations in the use of terminology and of methodology, there have been advances in the field of assessment. These include the recognition that an assessment of patient qual- ities on their own is not enough, that the other aspects of the equation—the analyst, the fit between the two, and the nature of the model of psychoanalysis—all need to be taken into account. There have also been advances in the way in which the assess- ment meeting itself is conducted, with more emphasis on the transference and countertransference and the notion of giving the patient some sense of what is to come in the analytic experience. This is both an advance and a reflection of the changes in psycho- analytic thinking: that is, that the patient is an active participant in the assessment just as he is in the analysis—part of a dyad, not the passive recipient of a recommendation or interpretations.

The way in which this review has been structured, singling out aspects of the assessment procedure for consideration, mirrors the problems in this field. The ingredients can be—if not measured— taken out and prepared, looked at, criticized; but in the final analysis any assessment is a combination of all these aspects, put together in a particular way by a particular assessor. To articulate that is an impossible task, influenced as we know we are by intuition, not to say by our own unconscious processes.

CHAPTER TWO

Where referrals come from and some links with general practice

Judith Barnard

> " *Would you tell me please, which way I ought to go from here?"*
>
> Lewis Carroll, *Alice's Adventures in Wonderland*

T he public view of psychoanalytic psychotherapy is mixed with much understandable confusion, and within the profession there is often fierce debate on theoretical differences. On reflection, it is rather remarkable that there are so many individuals working with therapists in a reasonably settled and painstaking endeavour to understand themselves. The majority of these people discover that therapy provides them with an opportunity to explore and alter the rigid patterns of their lives.

Sometimes it takes a long time to begin; one person had the telephone number crumpled up in a pocket for four years before yet another crisis pushed him to find the courage to ring the organization. There are obviously many different contacts and networks through which therapists are found, but in this chapter I try to outline the various ways in which people come to the Clinical Service of the British Association of Psychotherapists (BAP).

I then consider these ways in detail, particularly the link with medicine and the primary health care teams. I was a general practitioner for many years and now work as a therapist, so I am looking at this subject from a dual perspective.

When people telephone the BAP, they are asked where they live and how they heard about the organization; a note is made on whether the caller is a man or a woman. The number of female callers tends to be about double that of males, though in recent years more men than before have made enquiries. Over the years roughly a third of those who ring the organization contact an assessor for a consultation; about a third of those who are seen start in therapy. Some of the individual assessors change, but the pattern is constant.

It is interesting to wonder about what happens to those who do not contact an assessor or who make no further contact after having the consultation. Sometimes there are clues from people if they get in touch much later. For some, the act of "doing" something and acknowledging a problem is enough for the time being; they may shelve it, think about it, take some action, or turn to others. Sometimes there has been no idea of what psychotherapy would entail; for example, the thought of regular meetings, of months or years of therapy, is impossible to contemplate. It seems out of proportion, and "things are not that bad". For many there is a difficulty about fees, and for some the expectation is of low financial outlay, a sort of extension of the National Health Service. Some people resent paying fees for a matter that is seen to be connected with health and welfare. There are also many who simply have little money, and this points out the real need to subsidize more low-cost therapy.

For others, the thought of an assessment or preliminary consultation is daunting. Where turbulent feelings are involved, often at a time of crisis, one longs for a sympathetic person just to be there. If feelings of emptiness and depression are overwhelming, there can be great hesitation about seeking help from anyone. The Clinical Service provides an opportunity to explore these anxieties, and usually an assessment appointment is offered within two weeks. The rational process of finding therapy can be reassuring for people, but sometimes what emerges is profound anxiety that they will have to "perform", as in some kind of examination.

Some do not want an assessment, for other reasons: they do not feel they need one, or perhaps they have seen another professional person recently. It is important to acknowledge and discuss this, because it is really difficult to tell your story repeatedly, particularly when you are feeling vulnerable. This point also applies to the wider issue of referring someone on—for example, when a counsellor sends someone to us for an assessment for intensive therapy, or when an assessor refers someone to a therapist. Complicated feelings of loss and rejection may be there in connection with these changes, and they need to be addressed.

Geographical proximity to an assessor also makes a difference; ten years ago people travelled considerable distances to a therapist, and some still do, but it is now more difficult, and many are anxious about job insecurity and taking time off work. It may be stating the obvious, but a good local network of assessors and therapists is an important factor in a smooth referral system, and the links made through the Clinical Service are of great value in building this. Sometimes the association is telephoned as one of a list of numbers to see what may be offered. It is useful to have some knowledge of other organizations, both analytic and non-analytic; the experience of those dealing with the first enquiry and local knowledge both help to guide people along an appropriate route either before or after a consultation.

The Clinical Service generally receives around a thousand enquiries each year; these come from a variety of sources, and the numbers fluctuate over time. The largest group over several years, about a fifth of the calls, sometimes more, is made up of people who say they have found the organization in books, magazines, papers, and directories. This underlines the importance of having well-informed literature in circulation; the huge surge in therapies of all kinds is confusing enough for those of us who work in the field, let alone those who are looking for something and do not know where to start.

The next-largest group consists of those who have heard of therapy through relatives, friends, or colleagues who may have been in therapy themselves and feel they have benefited from it. Sometimes in a close relationship, the ripples of change in one person affect another in a way that is disturbing, and they will seek therapy for themselves. Others in this group are working or training to work in jobs involving mental health. Similar numbers of people used to be referred to the BAP by their GPs, health centre staff, or hospitals, but this section has dwindled; I consider this in more detail later. There is another important network of direct referral from doctors and other health workers through colleagues working together in the NHS. There are also people who will not ask the doctor for help because they find she is not interested, always prescribes drugs, or knows the family "too well". The issue of notes and confidentiality is a real and growing problem, not only in medical record-keeping; this is another reason often given for not consulting a doctor.

At one time, large numbers of people telephoned having heard about the organization through the radio or television. The result varies depending on who is broadcasting at the time and their views about psychotherapy: a popular and trusted figure will be seen to be offering hope and help to many. Individuals who approach us following broadcasts often decide not to commit themselves to regular therapy at this stage. They may come for a consultation and find this useful in itself. I remember one young woman who did not contact me again after a consultation but who recommended me to a friend two years later because it had helped her. The rest who telephone are from a dozen or so sources—counsellors, social services, colleagues in allied organizations and professions, also other groups and professions. For example, some businesses are aware of and concerned about the problem of stress. A few referrals come from astrologers, and a significant number say that they "cannot remember" or "just knew about the BAP".

So, as has been shown, people come to us from many different sources, and it is important to continue to think about improving links for those who could benefit. One problem is how to foster a sensible general view about psychotherapy in a climate where the connection with "mental illness" is still shunned and there is so much misunderstanding and debate about whether therapy is a good or a bad thing. Some media reporting gives a picture of counselling—and particularly psychotherapy—as an invasive process suggested as a solution for everything and encouraging dangerous dependence. This can cause understandable anxiety and antagonism. There are so many different approaches mushrooming under the guise of therapy that it is difficult for people to know which of them have a sound basis.

There are sections within the population nowadays that regard illness of any kind as an interruption in a series of busy arrangements. They want a fast cure, so it is a disappointment for them to find that therapy is not going to offer this and that the answer is not "given to you". In an increasingly materialistic society, there is a growing tendency to demand personal satisfaction as though it were a commodity. It is difficult for a doctor to practice and communicate on any kind of wavelength with people who, for example, telephone and demand a visit for a child who has had a fever for twenty-four hours but must be seen between two and three in the afternoon because the family is going shopping. Similarly, one meets unrealistic demands for therapy—wanting a therapist just down the road, for example, who will be available for a few weeks at five-thirty on a Tuesday.

However, there are also many people genuinely seeking something that may revive a feeling of meaning and vitality in their lives. In the struggle to be "normal" in present-day life, there can be a loss of common sense and a loss of the feeling of being connected to a world wider than ourselves. It seems to be human nature to resist exploring unconscious processes and the capacity for symbolic thinking, as though they were frightening aliens. After all, defences develop in the first place as a protection against the unbearable. Defences must be respected, and this understandable resistance to examining them is still an important factor in the general ambivalence about pursuing therapy.

Konrad Lorenz (1963), who has been described as the father of ethology, wrote about this resistance in his book, *On Aggression*. He says,

> Science is not to blame for men's lack of self knowledge. Giordano Bruno went to the stake because he told his fellow men that they and their planet were only a speck of dust in a cloud of countless other specks. When Charles Darwin discovered that men are descended from animals they would have been glad to kill him, and there was certainly no lack of attempts to silence him. When Sigmund Freud attempted to analyse the motives of human social behaviour and to explain its causes from the subjective psychological side, but with the

method of approach of true natural science, he was accused of
irreverence, blind materialism and even pornographic tendencies. Humanity defends its own self esteem with all its might,
and it is certainly time to preach humility and try seriously to
break down all obstructions to self knowledge. [p. 192]

Some of these points apply to the gulf between psychoanalytic
psychotherapy and the medical profession, a gulf that is still there
despite efforts on both sides to lessen the gap. Since so many
people consult a doctor about problems that could be helped by
psychotherapy, this is a sad state of affairs. One positive development is that there are now more counsellors and therapists
working in GP surgeries, though there still needs to be more regu-
lation and an understanding about different qualifications and
approaches.

In recent years, some of the changes in the NHS have caused
strain and low morale among professionals. They are overwhelmed by too many rules and regulations from management
on the one hand, and by high expectations, misery, and illness
from the patients on the other. The pace and climate of work in a
surgery have never been conducive to reflective thought about the
individual unless extra time was made, and this is even less possible now. General practitioners are being idealized as the leaders
of a primary-care–led health service and denigrated by being expected to meet impossible demands. No wonder, then, that on a
daily basis many doctors may react irritably to the mention of
stress and to patterns of disturbed behaviour that are freely acted
out and seem to have no answer.

The work, with GPs, of Michael Balint and others has influenced many doctors to think in more depth about the therapeutic
relationship. However, there have always been some barriers to
referrals from this source. Private treatment was, and to a degree
still is, seen as something apart and includes complicated issues of
"being cared for". People can become very attached in both positive and negative ways to the doctor and the general practice
"family", either during illness or for support nearly all the time!
Doctors can be quite possessive about their patients, and they
naturally wish to make their referrals to trusted and qualified colleagues. The problem is that many of these colleagues, including

psychiatrists, do not have any interest in the different way of thinking involved in psychoanalytic psychotherapy. Kenneth Sanders, a psychoanalyst who worked as a GP, has shown in his book (1986) that a psychoanalytic approach to family medicine does have a place and can be both relevant and interesting.

Freud and Jung both wrote about doctors and psychoanalysis in rather similar ways. Freud (1926e) wrote at some length, and with dry humour, about doctors and the place for treatment, or lack of it, for neuroses. He made the point that a medical training is more or less the opposite of what is needed as a preparation for psychoanalysis. In the same chapter he says, "Doctors whose interest has not been aroused in the psychical factors of life are all too ready to form a low estimate of them and to ridicule them as unscientific" (p. 231). He expressed pessimism about his work being more acceptable in the future. Jung (1933) wrote about how often the power of the relationship between doctor and patient is ignored and how important a factor it is in the healing process. He says (of doctors):

> Again, we so commonly underestimate the deeper aspects of the human psyche that we hold self-examination or preoccupation with ourselves to be almost morbid. We evidently suspect ourselves of harbouring unwholesome things all too reminiscent of a sick-room. [p. 59]

It is becoming more difficult for specialist knowledge to be shared. So many facts are now known in so many fields that not only is it impossible to "see the wood for the trees" but to see the tree for the twigs. There seems also to be a universal human need to find "The Answer", which is partly to do with curiosity and creativity and partly perhaps to do with finding an identity, status, and security in the world. Unfortunately, this often leads to closed schools of thought and a suspicion of the unknown.

Scientific investigation has developed along lines that lead to amazing precision in observing and measuring all sorts of detail, but it tends to ignore or dismiss that which cannot be defined within present limits. It is not known in these scientific terms how psychoanalytic psychotherapy works; the principles of a retraining process as in behaviour and cognitive therapy are sometimes more acceptable in modern medicine. The need for scientific accuracy, which we demand and welcome, pushes out other vital aspects of healing. The importance of feelings, emotional life, and sometimes plain good manners is often badly neglected.

Yet it has always been known that there is much in the practice of medicine that is "unscientific". In a psychotherapeutic consultation, we know that it is necessary to be aware of unconscious communication and other unspoken communication. In the GP surgery, it is important to develop this "sixth sense", which includes knowledge of disease patterns. It is often not possible to make exact diagnoses for the problems seen in this setting, and this awareness helps one to be alert to the possibility of serious illness when the pathology is not obvious. Children are more in touch with these communication faculties than many adults. One repeated experience I had in the surgery was to see a baby or young toddler suddenly stop the play in which he was engrossed and wave goodbye just before his mother and I realized that we were about to end our meeting.

These considerations extend to the division between mind and body. Sometimes it is important to remember that to divide ourselves thus is another contrivance of human thought and holds the same risk of splitting and seeing things in black and white. We still hear "it is psychological"—with the inference that it is bad or less worthy than the "physical"—from many people, including doctors, and we may hear "he is somatizing" from therapists, in the same tone of voice. So many interesting things that can happen to individuals get lost somewhere in-between, sometimes with disastrous consequences and missed diagnoses. The confusion of ideas increases when a previously well-defended, psychologically disturbed person begins to get better but succumbs to minor infections, which may be seen as a healthier alternative.

For practical purposes there has to be classification. However, one can look at it with a holistic approach, making it easier to consider the great variety of problems that we see. In a human being, the infinitely complex systems involving psyche and soma are in constant movement with each other and with the outside world. There is nothing that happens in the mind that is not somewhere represented in the body, and vice versa; it is a matter of degree. From this point of view, illness can be approached without the separation that persecutes patients as well as doctors and therapists. Such a concept can encompass all relevant specialist knowledge as well as different treatment approaches, and many conditions can be considered as a whole, such as some eating disorders and chronic fatigue syndrome.

Everyone knows how external stress has an overall effect and how it can lead to irritability, general exhaustion, or illness. Research into the functioning of the immune and endocrine systems, for example, is demonstrating these matters and showing us how immensely complicated they are. Equally, internal stress from past difficulties makes people vulnerable, and those who are experiencing deep internal conflict suffer increased morbidity and mortality. There can be a continuum between these states; from the ups and downs of ordinary life to the severe disruption of irreversible organized illness, with its attendant opportunity for regression. For each person health depends on many factors: genetic, environmental, as well as that person's internal and external reality.

Part of the basis of both medical work and psychotherapy is to try to contain anxiety, felt as such or experienced as physical tension, sometimes of desperate proportions. The two worries for most people when they feel the need to consult a professional about themselves are: "Will the problem be put right, and will I be treated well as a person?" This was touchingly conveyed by an 8-year-old patient of mine, who woke up one morning covered with chickenpox. "Get me to Dr Banana", he anxiously ordered his mother, "she will take these spots away".

In considering a psychotherapeutic approach we can also think along a continuum, starting from the relief of "getting something off one's chest" to a friend, to the possibility of a discussion with a GP or social worker, to supportive counselling or the more focused work of brief therapy, right through to in-depth work exploring the internal world in intensive psychoanalytic psychotherapy. Nearly everyone can find some sort of support from talking about how they feel to a person whom they trust. If anxiety is contained, the individual with a physical illness may be freer to get better. For example, after a visit to an older person with a severe infection, I have sometimes left "carrying" a feeling of gloom and pessimism; having conveyed this emotional burden of profound malaise and the spoken or unspoken fear of dying to the "doctor who understands", the patient starts to recover. I think that these instances show the surprising potential for change in many people rather than any particular pathology. Sometimes it is the patient who is emotionally healthy who can use the doctor in this way. There is, of course, a difference between this and long-term psychoanalytic work, where the reliability of the therapist and the setting are again part of the foundation for change, even if there is scant appreciation of this for long periods of time.

Much fascinating work has been done in the field of study of psychosomatic medicine. Change and development are rapid, and mentioning even a little about such a vast subject is difficult; it could be said that we all frequently experience psychosomatic symptoms. The connection between early life experience, illness, and emotional difficulty has been explored in detail. The recent great increase in knowledge from research in genetics is revealing more about inherited factors in personality and illness. The intricacy of the relationship between "nature and nurture" shows that in some ways the more we discover, the less we know. In his book on the holistic approach to various cancers, Professor Patrice Guex (1989), a Swiss psychiatrist, writes: "But all is not yet clear. For certain people, emotional inhibition and the capacity to develop a cancer may both result from genetic factors and need not be in a causal relationship" (p. 8). I have observed that in some patients with cancer there is a similar pattern of behaviour and denial; this has been different from the patterns in other patients with serious life-threatening disease.

The label of psychosomatic disease is sometimes still applied in an over-simplified way to the group of illnesses called the "Chicago 7" (bronchial asthma, gastric ulcer, essential hypertension, rheumatoid arthritis, ulcerative colitis, neurodermatitis, thyrotoxicosis). Stress may be significant in these conditions as in many others, but the aetiology is more varied than was first thought. Ulcerative colitis is mentioned often in analytic writing, but it is not very common in the community as a whole. Peptic ulceration has often been due to side-effects from anti-inflammatory drugs, rather than stress, in recent years, and the bronchospasm of asthma is caused by many factors. To illustrate this simply, one can imagine two different children, with asthmatic tendencies, each going to spend the night with a friend. The first, confident but with allergies, wakes wheezing in the night because the spare blanket is musty with house dust mite or the hamster is doing his nightly round on the wheel and spreading fur particles. The second, without known allergies, wheezes because it is one of his responses to anxiety about being away from home. The first may have deeper emotional difficulties, which could possibly affect his allergic response or not; both may develop further anxiety about the condition, which exacerbates it or makes them want to stay at home always, or not. Within limits, some children go around apparently unaware that they are making a breathing noise like an orchestra tuning up, and some are uncomfortable and terrified by slight spasm; there are endless variations.

Only a minority of psychotherapeutic consultations are sought for physical symptoms alone, and, of course, the approach in each case is to find out about the inner experience, including feelings about any illness. However, I think that the listener who has no awareness of biological variation risks distorting the situation as much as the one who denies that emotional factors are significant. There is also the danger of reducing physical symptoms to somatic causation in a way that underestimates their significance.

To look at another area, much ill health in a community is caused by infection; this has always been the case, and many illnesses thrive in overcrowded conditions, particularly amongst the young and the old. The very varied symptoms, which may not seem to be connected, are often rather trivialized or dismissed. We only have to think back a hundred years to remind ourselves how many children died and how much shorter was the average lifespan. Many diseases are now controlled, but viral illness in general is not; again, many factors, including psychological ones, can be involved in individual susceptibility and recovery.

One of our new young doctors was inspired by the Balint movement, as it came to be called, but he lacked tact and judgement. He started asking many patients what they had really come about—and they all rushed back to their boring old doctor, who was ineffective but who at least listened to their symptoms! It may sound ridiculous to say that illness makes people ill, but that is often where one starts and it has to be recognized before a new direction can be introduced.

In summary, the assessment for psychoanalytic psychotherapy is an attempt to discover whether the person who is interested, who is troubled, or who is caught up in more serious emotional conflict or physical problems can make use of this approach. The necessary starting points are motivation and the ability to look inside themselves for some answers. The assessment consultation also aims to use psychoanalytic understanding to see whether it would be contraindicated or pointless to start and, if so, to suggest an alternative. There are some people who might benefit from deeper therapy at some future date, but who need care and supportive therapy in the present; many psychoanalytic psychotherapists are experienced in working in this way. For example, someone recently bereaved, a new mother, or a person trying to cope with acute physical illness and complicated treatment may be in this group. Assessment cannot be an exact or certain process, but if psychoanalytic psychotherapy could be considered more often, the patchwork quality of referrals might be changed and widened to a more fluid network.

CHAPTER THREE

The difference between diagnosis and assessment in psychoanalytic psychotherapy

Anne Tyndale

"He merely told the unhappy Present to recite the Past"

W. H. Auden, "In Memory of Sigmund Freud"

Diagnosis identifies disease through investigating symptoms. An assessment is a judgement about whether someone who asks for psychoanalytic psychotherapy is going to be able to use this form of treatment. In making a diagnosis, a doctor concerns himself with illness; in making assessments, we are equally concerned with health. It is essential that a patient should have a sufficiently strong personality to undergo self-scrutiny and to tolerate the pain, disappointments, regrets and readjustments that inevitably follow such an exploration. In 1948, Kubie had warned that psychoanalysis was sometimes offered to patients on the basis of magical hopes rather than a realistic appraisal of the limitations of this form of treatment. Garelick (1994) observed that general practitioners making the most suitable referrals for psychoanalytic psychotherapy were those who had had no experience of psychotherapy themselves. Opinion based on informed judgement is the essence of both a good diagnosis and a good assessment; to recommend psychotherapy for others on the basis of an experience in which idealizations have not been worked through is dangerous.

The purpose of psychotherapy

The purpose of psychotherapy is to help the patient to disentangle an inner world, which has been created during childhood, from the shared reality of the outer world. Ways of self-protection that at one time seemed necessary to infant and child, who experienced the world as a dangerous or unfriendly place, are often in adult life put to inappropriate use. They deprive a person of the fulfilments arising from trusting relationships and a confidence in his own abilities. As Freud (1919h) discovered, many patients compulsively bring about the repetition of failure and trauma, which originally felt so unbearable that they believed they could only survive if it were undone. Others have turned away from the world in despair and fury, living on self-created islands populated by characters of their own making. Yet others severely limit their chances of making the most of opportunities by doing all they can to avoid feeling psychic discomfort or pain. Such pain may be transformed into incapacitating physical illness or destructive action taken to circumvent feeling. An assessor has to judge whether, in the reliable safety of the analytic frame, a patient will be able to take the risk of mourning previous losses and disappointments and altering his view of himself and the world.

Treatment alliance

There must always be an alliance between a helper and the one helped. It is impossible to free a dog entangled in a barbed-wire fence if all it does is bite you. Some of the prerequisites for forming a "treatment alliance" are the same for a diagnostician and the patient as for an assessor and the person seeking psychotherapy.

In both cases, the patient must accept the need for help and see the helper as someone willing and likely to work to his advantage. During the course of psychotherapy, this perception will undoubtedly fluctuate and may sometimes recede from sight, but if it is not there at the beginning there is poor chance that the treatment will be worthwhile. For instance, a patient may have come to the assessment only to prove that he has no allies in the world. He will see the assessor as hostile and demeaning and may triumphantly wish to denigrate all that the assessment offers. With this unconscious need to use the therapy in order to take revenge on figures from the past, it is unlikely that the patient will gain much benefit.

Tyson and Sandler (1971) list several abilities that an assessor should look for when considering whether a patient is able to form a treatment alliance. They mention a capacity to observe oneself as if one were another—perhaps rather a tall order before beginning therapy—and possession of ego strengths that normally develop outside the sphere of neurotic conflict. These include an ability to organize oneself sufficiently to keep appointments, and a certain level of intelligence (though as these authors point out, a facility for abstract thinking is far less important than a readiness to use insight). Patients must also be capable of keeping to a contract concerning the fifty-minute session, paying regularly, and not taking destructive action against therapist or property. To this extent, a therapist must be able to trust the patient—trust that is not normally relevant to the diagnostician's brief with a patient.

It is clearly important that patients should have confidence in the skill of any professional whose help they seek. This is very different from establishing the kind of trust required to bring about psychological change, which can only be acquired through experience. In 1905 Freud was already pointing out the need to analyse a hostile transference, which is bound to emerge in any of our patients. Too much trust from the start may be a counterindication for therapy.

"I trusted you implicitly the moment I met you", said Mr C, who during three years of therapy allowed no negative feelings to enter into his perception of his therapist. He was very afraid of experiencing the terrifying absence and hatred he had felt in his relationship with his mother. Inevitably, however, the therapist proved imperfect, and, fearing he had lost everything, Mr C broke off the treatment.

Too little trust may also be a warning sign in assessment. If a patient shows a great deal of anxiety about confidentiality or the integrity of the therapist as a person, or anticipates hostility from the surrounding world, he may not be able to bear his vulnerability in the analytic situation.

Trust is also needed for the capacity to regress, which is essential for a patient to work through feelings surrounding childhood traumas. He needs to be able to experience the fears of his earlier life and the wishes and hopes that may have been essential to save him from despair. Sometimes an assessor will have the chance to point out to the patient how at one moment he seems to see the assessor as someone ready to exploit or criticize and, at another, someone offering salvation. Both fears and wishes from the past are thus brought under observation through the way he relates to the therapist. This gives him the opportunity to see how psychoanalytic psychotherapy may help him to weigh up these opposing views, which have been with him from an early age, against a third, more realistic view. Nevertheless, we cannot always tell from this kind of insight how much a patient will be able to risk entering a world of infantile feeling in the presence of a therapist who maintains the link with reality. In contrast, a tendency to regress may be unhelpful to a diagnostician wanting to discuss and treat illness at an adult level with a patient; for instance, it might lead to agreement that the patient later regrets.

Some assessors feel that unless a patient is committed to therapy from the beginning, his chances of seeing it through to a satisfactory level are minimal. During an assessment, problems about commitment need to be understood as far as possible and an opinion formed about the likelihood of gradually solving them. It may be that the patient's present suffering, or interest in discovering more about himself, is not sufficient to motivate him to give up other pursuits in order to make time and space for therapy. In this case he probably will not sustain his part in a difficult process, one that requires much hard work. There are, however, other reasons for difficulty about commitment; for instance, anxieties about being wanted or not wanted (the therapist's commitment), an inability to make decisions in general, or conflicts about owning up to need. Most important of all may be a fear about what will be discovered. It is inevitable that a patient coming for either a diagnosis or assessment will have some ambivalence about whether or not he really wants the knowledge he is asking for. However, such anxieties may be worked through over a period of time, during which the patient will become more, rather than less, committed.

It is important for an assessor presented with a patient in great distress to keep a firm hold on the present reality. However suitable, psychologically speaking, a patient may seem, unless certain external circumstances are favourable, the treatment cannot be offered. The patient must, for instance, live within reach of a suitable therapist. He must have enough money to pay for therapy over a long period of time if necessary. Equally important is the presence of friends or family who can help to sustain him in the outer world when his inner one threatens to overwhelm him. If the therapy is going to call for sacrifices from other members of a family who are unwilling to meet them, it is likely to break down.

History and memories

Making an assessment is, therefore, like diagnosis, partially a fact-finding exercise; often, however, the most significant "facts" are not verifiable by external evidence, they are reported from the patient's point of view. For instance, when I asked a patient about her earliest memory, she said: "This can't be true, but I remember my mother told me to gather some flowers and was angry because I picked them." The truth of the statement need not concern us here; what matters is that the patient felt that she had been unjustly treated by an inconsistent mother. The memory is probably a "screen memory", containing within it many incidents of a similar nature. This patient had already let the assessor know how vital it would be for a future therapist to keep strictly to the analytic boundaries.

A person's history is important in assessment and diagnosis, though each is concerned with different aspects. Diagnostically, a patient's genetic history is often of vital significance, and this will be noted not only by doctors but also by psychotherapists. In making an assessment for psychoanalytic psychotherapy, experiences of early relationships, traumatic events, and how the patient has dealt with normal psychological changes throughout childhood and adolescence are important. When considering a patient's history, neither doctors nor psychotherapists can risk the omission of significant factors; questions need to be asked. Such questions might be about previous psychiatric or hospital treatment, or perhaps, "the worst time in your life". However, facts about the past provide more determining evidence in diagnosis than in assessment. The crucial consideration in assessment is how the patient sees himself in relation to his history and the present day. If he is unable to consider that there may be any links between the past and present, his capacity to benefit from insight offered, or to use the transference, may be impossibly limited.

Although necessary for diagnosis, questions that call for factual answers may be counterproductive if what we are seeking is understanding of how a patient thinks, his capacity for free association, and his ability to differentiate inner from outer reality. One of the most difficult aspects of assessment is the necessity to combine some questioning with giving the patient the space, time, and opportunity to talk about his inner world and thus to experience the way psychoanalytic psychotherapy works. At the same time, he gives the therapist some insight into his hopes and anxieties through recounting dreams, events, or fantasies that convey a picture of himself on a deeper level. His expectations of how his material will be received can also be explored, helping him to understand the unique opportunity provided by psychoanalytic psychotherapy to discover the influences of childhood relationships through the transference relationship with the therapist.

Missing facts may make accurate diagnosis impossible. To a therapist making an assessment, however, they are sometimes of just as much use as the information offered. After an hour and a half with a professionally qualified young man, I pointed out that he had told me nothing yet about his mother. "What should I need to mention her for?", he said. As he was leaving the room he turned around and stated emphatically: "If my wife ever left me, I'd kill myself." He had let me know enough about a terrifyingly abandoning internal mother to make me think very carefully about the kind of referral I would need to consider.

The aims of patient and therapist in psychoanalytic psychotherapy

Objective considerations are therefore only one aspect of making an assessment. Unlike the diagnostician, who is concerned with judgement based on fact, the assessor must also pay careful attention to the patient's wishes and intentions.

As I have already shown, cooperation is an essential factor in psychoanalytic psychotherapy, and nothing can be achieved if the two parties have disparate aims. The assessor's task is to give the patient some idea of the purpose of psychotherapy and to help him decide if this is what he wants.

Most people seek therapy in order to feel better: "I looked in the mirror and saw a fine young lady." This moving dream of the previous night was recounted to me by a young woman of very low self-esteem. However, in 1966 Greenacre warned that the zeal to cure overvalues psychoanalytic therapy in comparison with other treatments. Freud veered between thinking that research aspects of psychoanalysis were more important than treatment ones, and vice versa. In 1912 he concluded that the most successful cases were those in which the analyst proceeded with no purpose in view (neither scientific nor therapeutic).

Research and treatment are often combined in medical treatment, and there is usually no hesitation in referring a patient to a doctor with a special interest in his condition; this may not always be to the patient's advantage as far as psychotherapy is concerned. In order to use this type of treatment, however, patients must be prepared to research into themselves. An assessor has to find out if the adult who presents himself in the consulting-room wants to know more about himself in order to foster development (Klauber, 1981). He must therefore accept that there are conflicts within himself of which he is ignorant, and which prevent his life from progressing. Unconsciously, he may hope for very many other things, such as finding the perfect parent in the therapist, everlasting admiration, or protection from all pain.

Sometimes the aims of a deprived or damaged infant self are so consuming that the stated aim is squashed out of sight; in such cases, we might consider that the patient will get such little satisfaction from self-examination that he will be unlikely to have the capacity to carry it out.

A middle-aged man, coming with the declared intention of understanding himself, spent nearly an hour and a half telling me about numerous past therapists, all of whom, so he said, had not only fallen in love with him but also acted upon their feelings. He was soon saying, despite knowing he was only with me for an assessment, that he would like to see me five times a week or more. His wish to be in a controlling, exciting, and inseparable entanglement with a therapist was so strong that I thought it unlikely he would be able to make enough space for the reflection necessary to fulfil his stated aim.

Another patient, perhaps coming because his GP has sent him, may spend the assessment talking about physical symptoms of various kinds and be unable to consider that these have any psychic meaning. He wants the symptoms magically removed. It is the task of the assessor to try to help him to see that the body and mind are closely linked; this enables him to understand that one of the aims of therapy is to help him to take responsibility for his symptoms. He may or may not wish to do this.

Some patients come for assessment in order to shore up their defences against self-knowledge. They may complain that their lives are intolerable because of the behaviour of a child or spouse, as if it has nothing to do with them. In this case, part of the purpose of the assessment is to enable them to see how anxious they may be about confronting what they fear or dislike in themselves. Perhaps they do not want to do this and so do not return. On the other hand, they may feel greatly relieved that someone is prepared to consider, with them, problems in themselves that they feared were unmanageable. Betty Joseph (1983) and John Steiner (1993) have written about the difference between wanting to be understood and gaining understanding. Nina Coltart (1992) accepts that the wish to be nurtured and understood is important, but it is not, she emphasizes, therapeutic unless accompanied by the understanding of projections and working through. In extreme form, an unwillingness to gain understanding amounts to a refusal to take responsibility. Such passivity may undermine the patient's ability to make use of being understood in a way that can lead to change. This difficulty does not arise when making a diagnosis, because self-understanding does not have the same place. It is important that during an assessment the therapist should give the patient the opportunity to think for himself to see whether he is able to use his own capacities, or whether panic or a wish to hand over all responsibility to someone else causes him to project vital ego strengths into the therapist. Betty Joseph (1983) alerts us to patients who unconsciously try to persuade the therapist to act out part of their own ego or superego; if we do this without observation, she says, we are often repeating situations from their past. This may happen in an assessment, and subsequent discussion can help us to gauge the level of passivity in the patient.

All therapists have met an adult patient harbouring within himself a resentful and sometimes despairing child or adolescent, who feels that no one has ever appreciated the horror of his life. It is often essential that he should feel listened to in order to be able to make some sense of himself and his history. Until this happens, the capacity to use understanding to alter his present life cannot be found. Trial interpretations in assessment may therefore appear to fall on stony ground, but perhaps the soil is not yet fertile rather than hopelessly barren.

The aim of psychoanalytic psychotherapy is to increase a patient's understanding of himself, but what the patient does with self-knowledge should not be predicted or interfered with. Wilfred Bion's (1962) pronouncement that the analyst should have no "memory or desire" applies equally to assessors as to those offering treatment. If there is an expectation about how the patient will experience the assessment and what it might mean to him, true exploration and freedom of choice are already limited.

A diagnosis, on the other hand, is usually designed to lead to a definite plan, unless there is found to be nothing wrong with the patient. In this case, the diagnosis itself may bring relief. If, after an assessment, a patient decides there is nothing wrong with him, he may also sense temporary relief, but it can be a sign of "flight into health", an avoidance of facing hard truths. An assessment, however, can constitute a therapeutic experience of a different kind. I suggested to a woman that I thought the difficulties she had in taking any risks, and therefore in fulfilling her potential, might be connected with a feeling in adolescence of stepping out to face a frightening world with no one to back her up. A year later she returned asking for therapy, saying that following her assessment she had begun, for the first time, to think about herself in a way that made sense.

Understanding what is wrong

When making a diagnosis, the doctor looks for what is wrong: either illness, disease, or disability. Assessment for psychoanalytic psychotherapy also has to include a careful understanding of what is wrong with the patient. The removal of a symptom might be so urgent that it needs to be attended to by another form of treatment, possibly at the same time as the slow unravelling of its meaning through psychoanalytic psychotherapy. The mother of a young child told me she had such a fear of moths that, when she saw one in her baby's bedroom, she was unable to enter the room, even though the baby had been crying for some time. I referred her to a behavioural psychologist but thought that her need to displace a fear she could not face, onto moths, would inevitably lead to other symptoms occurring and that she should be referred to a psychoanalytic psychotherapist as well.

In another instance a young man came to see me two years after the death of his psychotic mother. He was afraid that, like his mother, he was turning away from life and was becoming withdrawn, apathetic, and confused. It was important to try to ascertain whether this patient was on the verge of a psychotic breakdown himself or whether he was identifying with a mother whose death he could not mourn. He appeared reflective, able to make links with the past, and interested in noticing how, even in the short space of the assessment, he tried to look after me, as he

DIAGNOSIS AND ASSESSMENT   57

always had his mother. I thought that if the second possible diagnosis was correct, he might gain much help from psychotherapy but he could not do this if his hold on reality was too tenuous to maintain the "as if" quality of the transference relationship. I therefore referred him to a psychiatrist for a further consultation.

Although it is impossible to uncover a person's psychopathology in one assessment, it is important when making a referral for the assessor to formulate, as accurately as possible, the level of the patient's disturbance. This gives a therapist the chance to decide whether to take on this kind of patient.

The combined task of diagnosis and assessment

The double task of making a diagnosis and deciding whether or not a patient can use the treatment we offer is not as cumbersome as it may seem. Our most vital "tool", which is different from the strictly medical ones, enables us to make an assessment while considering facts necessary for diagnosis. This tool is observing the way that the patient relates to us in the interview.

Mr P was an angular, brittle-looking man in his early 40s. He was conventionally dressed in a way that seemed to hide, rather than reveal, anything about his personality. He changed the time of his appointment, arrived an hour early, went away, and returned twenty minutes late. As he climbed my stairs, he made an aggressive remark about the size of the house and then asked some intrusive questions. I felt attacked, imposed upon, and not too keen to see him. At the same time, I had a strong feeling of unease. He sat down, and as we started to talk I found myself feeling sad, protective, and encouraging.

Mr P told me that he was seeking therapy because he had never had a sexual relationship with either a man or a woman, and he felt he was missing something important. He was born to an actress devoted to her career; her request for an abortion had been refused. "She only kept me because she had to", he said, and she never revealed the identity of his father. Now he found that if anyone showed signs of wanting him, he withdrew immediately. Towards the end of the interview he also told me he thought he had effeminate features that made him unacceptable to others.

Mr P's description of himself enabled me to make a diagnosis of his problems. He was an unwanted child, deprived of a mother who loved him and of a father. He now felt that no one else would want him and that he was physically abnormal; he therefore made it impossible for himself to find a partner. I noted that his anxiety about his body might be of a delusional nature, though there was nothing in his history indicative of psychosis. I concluded, therefore, that although Mr P functioned with a false self that probably concealed narcissistic or borderline pathology, he was not suffering from a mental illness, which would preclude the possibility of psychotherapy.

However, this useful formulation did not provide me with sufficient grounds for deciding whether or not the patient would be a suitable candidate for psychoanalytic psychotherapy. In order to make the assessment I turned to the patient's behaviour and my own response to it. First of all, I realized that he had communicated a great deal. The patient's intense anxiety about asking for help was displayed in his behaviour surrounding the time of the appointment. By changing the time originally he may have been unconsciously trying to find out how much I wanted to see him. Then, having given me a glimpse of his hungry longing by arriving early, he reversed the situation so that I was the one waiting and wanting him to arrive. He pushed me away by his attack about the stairs but let me know how much he wished for, more in fact than he could have, by his questions. Their demanding nature also indicated that he felt that he would never get anything unless he took it. He was thus letting me know about his wishes and fears and the defensive way in which he dealt with them. This showed that he had some hope that I might be able to understand his anxiety and to put up with his behaviour. Despite his life of self-deprivation, he was still open to the possibility of feeling wanted and therefore of change.

My compassionate feeling towards this angular, angry man

was also useful in making the assessment. Here was a vulnerable person needing protection and nurturing; in revealing to me a part of himself that felt helpless, he was giving some indication of an ability to regress in therapy sufficiently to bring about a healing change. My feeling of awkwardness in the countertransference, however, let me know of primitive defences used by this patient. He may have been wanting me to know how he felt with a mother for whom he was a nuisance. I also had to consider whether he had the capacity to contain anxiety, or whether his tendency to take action to avoid feeling, as he did by arriving early and then being late, might endanger both the therapy and himself.

This example shows how important it is in assessment to take note of a patient's presentation of himself, the way he behaves, and his effect on the therapist. We cannot, as in a diagnostic procedure, rely on symptoms for information. In their very useful article on assessment, Tyson and Sandler (1971) give examples of attempts by Knapp et al. (1960) and Malan (1967) to use categories of symptoms as indications for suitability for psychoanalytic psychotherapy. They cite Kubie (1948), however, who points out that neurotic symptoms can arise from a great variety of psychopathological states. Anna Freud (1954) backs up Kubie's argument when she comments that there is no guarantee that two individuals with the same symptomatology will react similarly to the same technical procedure. Elizabeth Zetzel (1970) made the same point when she differentiated between the types of hysterical patient more or less suitable for psychoanalytic treatment; the nature of their relationships was a much better indicator than their symptoms.

The necessity to discuss
both diagnosis and assessment with the patient

There may be exceptional circumstances under which a doctor would not divulge to a patient coming to him for a diagnosis the nature of his illness. On the whole, however, it is generally agreed that if someone asks what is wrong with him, a physician has a duty to tell him. Often a patient coming for assessment for psychotherapy already has his own ideas about what is wrong with him and wants to tell the assessor. Sometimes he does not make a diagnosis but presents the psychotherapist with a collection of symptoms, which he may see as having nothing to do with his past history or internal world; he thinks that they have occurred by chance or because of the immediate circumstances of his life.

A patient's self-diagnosis should be listened to very carefully; it helps us to understand what he sees as the most important impediment in his life and is valuable in assessing the degree of insight he has already gained. It may coincide with the assessor's diagnosis, add to it, or differ from it. It is now the assessor's duty to give the patient an opinion about the nature of his difficulties in the context of his past and present life.

In Ogden's (1989) opinion it is more important in assessment to help the patient to recognize and understand transference thoughts than to put him at ease. Such recognition may be far more containing, and therefore ultimately comforting, than the creation of a cosy atmosphere. Similarly, an interpretation that is, in Klauber's (1981) terms, sensible and not mysterious helps to dispel hopes of a magic, omnipotent therapist from the beginning. It is often reassuring for a patient to understand how a diagnosis is reached; similarly, there is need to understand how an assessor arrives at interpretations.

Mrs X came asking for very low-cost therapy. During the course of the assessment she told me how, when she was a child, she had often visited friends' houses and secretly taken objects home. "It was as if I felt they belonged to me already", she said. With difficulty, she made sense of my interpretation that many of her conflicts arose from the unconscious feeling that she could take whatever she wanted in recompense for her deprived childhood. Her unwillingness to pay the full fee for therapy was part of the same problem. The assessment gave this patient a chance to understand how quickly she wanted to draw me into the sadness and fury of her relationship with figures of the past and how psychotherapy might help her to sort out her inner world from the external one. She was therefore in a position to make a judgement about whether she wanted to use this kind of treatment or not.

Is assessment useful?

A diagnosis is accepted to be a prerequisite for treatment, but questions often arise about the necessity or usefulness of assessments. Can we predict who will be able to make use of psychoanalytic psychotherapy? Limentani (1989) cautions assessors not to overvalue their own judgement. A psychotic transference, he states, is often difficult to predict; interaction and transference manifestations that occur at first interviews have nothing to do with the transference neurosis to come. He warns assessors that patients who they think will be able to make a firm treatment alliance may turn out to have a hard core of basic mistrust that constantly sabotages the therapy. On the other hand, too much caution, he says, might deprive a patient of psychotherapy as an essential lifeline.

Dr Limentani's words are wise. We cannot draw a map for anyone's journey through psychoanalytic psychotherapy, but, within our own limitations, we can make a careful judgement about the likelihood of a patient profiting from it. Klauber (1981) reminds us of the hope invested in psychoanalytic treatment and how the dependency, depression, and disturbance that inevitably arise in the course of it can affect family relationships and work. Along with Nina Coltart (1992), who warns us that psychoanalytic psychotherapy can be a waste of time and money, he also says it can cause harm. Assessing a patient's capacity to use this form of therapy is just as important a responsibility as making an accurate diagnosis of illness. If recommended ill-advisedly, it can have very serious consequences; at worst, it may even exacerbate disturbance.

CHAPTER FOUR

Once-weekly
or more intensive therapy

Judy Cooper and Helen Alfillé

"Experience has taught us that psycho-analytic therapy—the freeing of someone from his neurotic symptoms, inhibitions and abnormalities of character—is a time-consuming business"

Freud, 1937c, p. 216

T his quotation from Freud contains what is, in a sense, the basic assumption underlying an assessment. Psychotherapy offers no instant cure or magical solution. Human beings are notoriously averse to change—however much they may consciously be seeking it—and psychotherapy is about fundamental change. Whether one sees the goal of treatment in terms of gaining insight and working through, so that this new knowledge may be tested repeatedly; in terms of principally embellishing the creative or eradicating the destructive elements in a patient's psyche; or even in terms of providing a holding experience different from the original environmental failure, "The business of the analysis is to secure the best psychological conditions for the functioning of the ego; with that it has discharged its task" (Freud, 1937c, p. 250). To do this and in order to evaluate

63

what a patient needs, one must remember that the aim is not the elimination of all psychological conflict, as this would lead to complete stasis.

Having all these goals in mind, how do we decide on the intensity (i.e. the frequency) of the treatment to be offered? To shift someone's internal world, which often includes damaged and persecuting objects, towards introjecting a good object is bound to take time and involve considerable work.

In our view, there is a clear distinction between once-weekly therapy and more than once-weekly, whether this is two, three, four, or five times weekly. Whatever the number of sessions, the fundamental aims of the treatment do not differ much. However, the patient's experience of his therapy will be radically different depending on the frequency of his sessions. It must be pointed out that anything more than three times a week is theoretically considered psychoanalysis, and this frequency "produces a bias towards the primitive anxieties which emerge during the regression evoked by such intensity" (Bateman & Holmes, 1995, p. 24).

The assessor has a difficult task. Sometimes, once-weekly therapy is the treatment of choice; at other times, it can be a preparation for more intensive work. However, we are often constrained by the patient's unconscious ambivalence, which can become linked to reality-based difficulties associated with time, money, and location.

Most therapists will recognize the patient for whom once-weekly therapy is sufficient, where it can be therapeutic, preoccupying, but not obsessive. Others are able to use once-weekly therapy as an intensive experience; they can internalize the therapist and hold on to the process from week to week. Furthermore, for those who come to therapy knowing nothing about it, and for whom the idea of more than once a week would seem quite threatening, once-weekly sessions may be used as a period of preparation, almost a time of education: "It is not unusual for some individuals to become analysable in the course of time" (Limentani, 1989, p. 63). There are others who come anxious and possibly mistrustful, who may start with one session a week but increase the number when they and their therapist feel ready. A patient who was seen weekly for a year increased her sessions to three times weekly after a dream in which she started out on a dramatic journey by train. The engine had refused to start, but when it eventually did it went agonisingly slowly, gathering speed gradually. Both therapist and patient felt that she was ready for more intensive therapy.

However, we believe that there are two distinct groups of patients for whom once-weekly psychotherapy would be the treatment of choice. For severely damaged people, who nonetheless can use individual psychotherapy in private practice, the feared intimacy of more frequent, one-to-one sessions may feel unbearable; once a week offers a balance between being overwhelmed on the one hand, and abandoned on the other. The second group comprises patients who may be functioning perfectly adequately but have problematic areas that they want to explore and understand. An elderly patient came into once-weekly therapy because she needed someone to hear her life story in its entirety. She needed to integrate the traumatic events of her life with one person, in one place. Although she had managed her life well enough for eighty years, both she and her therapist were impressed with the insight gained through interpreting her dreams and associations, which led to her being able to see what her own masochistic part had been in contributing to these painful situations. The therapy reached deeper levels than expected but was containable and not overwhelming for this woman, whose ego was strong enough to hold on to the process from week to week.

Perhaps the issue of whether to use the couch or chair is more likely to be raised by once-weekly patients, who may expect to use a chair for their therapy. Even with patients coming more frequently, some may feel the need to observe their therapist in a more interactive way, some may feel the need to be more in control, and some may be disturbed by hearing a disembodied voice. Of course, more primitive fears can emerge no matter what the frequency of therapy. A patient may need to keep his feet "on the ground", ready for flight or to feel grounded in reality. Lying on the couch may arouse fears of a seductive or aggressive attack.

Of course, as we have mentioned, there are external realities in the patient's life to be taken into consideration during the assessment. Moreover, the patient's priorities and motivation form part of the equation. There are various questions we need to bear in mind when assessing patients who are unwilling to consider coming more than once a week. Will it encourage game-playing, generating a play-acting feeling, of being both in and yet out of therapy, where it could become a tantalizing exchange? Each session may become an exciting encounter and remain a new experience, a defence against familiarity and closeness. In extreme cases, but not altogether uncommonly, patients may take great care with their appearance for their weekly session, which can become the focus for a tremendous amount of erotic energy. For example, one patient travelled from London to Nottingham each week for her therapy session, and her whole week became focused around this ritualized event.

With a busy life and only a once-weekly, fifty-minute session, it is very easy for a patient just to report on his daily activities. The session gets taken up with this verbal diary, and little time and space is left for reflection or deeper exploration: the patient is able to off-load and escape. Generally, it is difficult to hold on to what seemed important in the last session, a week ago. There may also be undue pressure having one session a week: for the patient, an expectation that something must be achieved each time, which is contrary to the tempo of long-term work; for the therapist, a pressure to be helpful and produce "the good interpretation".

It has been said by a patient who has experienced five-times-weekly psychoanalysis that an insight gained in her subsequent once-weekly psychotherapy could be exciting momentarily but that it seemed to be unsustainable for the whole week before her next session. The momentum had been lost. Equally painstaking work—whether once-weekly or more—must be done on lowering defences, only to have them reestablished quickly in the absence of a follow-up session immediate enough to encourage working through.

There are some cases where the assessor feels that once-weekly therapy is clearly contraindicated because the patient definitely requires more, and once-weekly sessions would prove totally inadequate. For instance, this might apply to the schizoid patient who is unable to register the therapist as a separate person either internally or externally, whose defence is to stay in the realm of the intellect, splitting off from his feelings. These patients would ideally need three sessions or more a week.

Because a week is a legitimate time-span of our making, therapy more than once a week helps to develop the transference relationship and to build up a continuity of experience conducive to our analytic work. It is for this reason that many analysts and therapists, even for twice-weekly therapy, prefer the sessions to be on consecutive days. This enables interpretations about breaks in the therapy, with the attendant separation anxiety, to be more relevant to the patient's experience. Moreover, intensive therapy allows the time and space for more reflective work; the patient feels more held, more involved in the process, and can hold on to the relevant issues. One may also need to consider what is manageable for the therapist; on occasions, it feels uncontainable to have to wait a week to continue the therapy.

However one looks at the goals of treatment—whether the aim is gaining insight and working through, providing an experience of primary holding (which Winnicott, 1954, defined as including the setting, the analyst, and the work), or reaching the depressive position—it is hard to achieve psychic change, particularly in once-weekly work. For deep analytic work, which invariably involves a degree of regression, intensive psychotherapy is imperative. In recommending intensive work, however, an assessor must consider the total life situation of the patient, ensuring that he has sufficient environmental holding to support him. It can be perilous for the patient, the therapist, and the treatment to have a regressed patient without any holding network.

As a result of our training with the British Association of Psychotherapists, our preference is for intensive, long-term work. For this, it is essential for us to be in touch with the primitive emotions of our inner world, so that as assessors we are careful to refer to those therapists who, we feel, can best articulate these areas of pre-verbal experience to their patients.

With the high expectations stemming from the plethora of choice on offer to people today in every area of life, with the erosion of the old structures of family and religion, many more people are searching for answers and a sense of self. Today's culture tends to encourage the idea of a "quick fix" and short-term magical solutions for deep-seated problems. By definition, this is anti-analytic. It is very often difficult for patients to understand the need for commitment to intensive work over a long period of time.

Patients coming through a clinical service tend to be a diverse cross-section. They are anxiously seeking help for any of a wide variety of difficulties. They may be motivated but not focused as to how psychotherapy could be helpful and what it could offer them. In the assessment consultation, the therapist needs to be able to focus, first, on the nature of the problems presented and what underlies this and whether these can be usefully explored in psychoanalytic psychotherapy, then on whether the patient, himself, can use psychotherapy. Finally, the frequency of sessions needs to be decided. In considering the intensity, we also need to be aware that the therapist should be able to survive the aggression of the patient: "You survive what I do to you as I come to recognise you as not-me" (Winnicott, 1968, p. 103).

A patient's story, including his history, memories, and all that makes up his internal and external world, is there to be explored. Unconscious patterns of behaviour will inevitably be repeated, no matter the intensity of treatment. However, the whole experience, the feeling of continuity, the depth at which work can take place, the level able to be reached in the unconscious, all these factors must be influenced by the frequency of sessions. Many therapists feel that to contain the psychotherapeutic endeavour in once-weekly sessions is much more difficult than in two or more sessions per week.

CHAPTER FIVE

The significance
of the opening story

Arna Davis

> "What part of the subject
> in what state
> situated where in space and time
> does what with what motivation
> to what part of the object
> in what state
> situated where in space and time
> with what consequences for the object and the subject"
>
> Dr Henri Rey's Model of thinking

There are innumerable ways of proceeding in an assessment interview, depending both on the assessor's way of working and on the problems presented by each individual patient. The assessor's task is to gather sufficient information to discover why this person is seeking help, what are his expectations of psychotherapy as a treatment for his problems, what are the key symptoms and difficulties that have made him take action, and why now. How can the patient's symptoms be used as unconscious communications leading to the uncovering of his healing potential?

Here, I limit myself to exploring the patient's opening story—in particular, how its communicative meaning can be used as one of the tools guiding the thinking, the formulating, and the decision-making process in the assessment interview. Obviously, the setting of the interview—the consulting-room—should be a safe and confidential space, with an atmosphere in which unconscious material can emerge uncontaminated by disturbances caused by the external reality of "an unsafe frame" (Langs, 1978).

Jung (1928) stressed that analysis is an art and not a scientific or technical procedure, his main emphasis being the need to adapt to the individual patient, and for the therapist to use his knowledge merely as hypotheses for possible explanations. What about assessment in psychotherapy—is it a science or an art? In the introduction to *The Art and Science of Assessment in Psychotherapy*, Mace (1995) states:

> Set alongside the ordinary work of psychotherapy, "assessment" carries an aura of heightened precision and objectivity. Researchers have made only modest contributions to validating criteria that could help assessors advise patients about therapeutic options, and have very little to say on how time given to assessment could be most effectively used. [p. 2]

Julia Kristeva (1983) has drawn our attention to the story as a text that can be analysed on a number of levels and understood as the product of many separate, but interconnecting strands. Bandler and Grindler (1975) suggest an underlying three-stage process of meaning in therapeutic metaphors: first, there is the surface structure of the storyline, the actual form of the story in words and actions; second, an associated deep structure of meaning which is indirectly relevant to the listener, being both specific and personal; and third, the recovered deep structure of meaning that is directly relevant to the listener. This in turn provides a bridge between the story and the listener's private inner world.

When listening to the patient, one pays attention to three aspects:

1. the descriptive or manifest content of the story;
2. the timing of telling and the context in which the story is told;

3.   the interactional structures, the tensions and conflicts, the unresolved divisions within the psyche, the inner drama, "the maximum pain" (Hinshelwood, 1995).

It is the understanding of the unconscious meaning of the story which allows a shift of perception or of emotional attitudes.

Jung (1928) asserted that analysis is a "dialectical process". By this he meant that there are two people involved, the implication being that the unconscious of both is involved. There is a two-way interaction between them, and the interaction becomes a centre of interest. The relationship is the key determinant of what is being observed. These unseen connections between what were previously thought to be separate entities are the fundamental elements of all creation. They form a pattern characteristic of that moment, which reveals its truth if the pattern can be read. He was interested in what is the story behind the story:

Psychotherapy is an encounter, a discussion between two psychic wholes, in which knowledge is used only as a tool. The goal is transformation. [para. 904]

In describing a psychodynamic formulation in assessing a patient for psychotherapy, Hinshelwood (1995) focuses on three areas of object relationships: the current life situation, the early infantile relations, and the transference relationship. In my formulations I am following similar lines, adding the opening story, within the context of the assessment process, as a communication, given to me by the patient, needing to be "de-coded" and translated (Langs, 1978).

Thus the assessment may be seen as a certain kind of dialogue, where the assessor's task is to draw out the patient's story by listening, asking questions, trying to understand, and making formulations, but holding to these lightly. The assessor is there to follow the patient's story, not to take it over.

The re-framing of the problem—the outcome and the recommendations to the patient, whether he is suitable for intensive analytic psychotherapy, or whether individual psychotherapy is the appropriate treatment for this patient—is based on what has been heard, seen, experienced, understood and thought about, within the context of the gathering of factual information. In this information gathering, one must pay attention to the interactions that have taken place in the interview—the transference–countertransference observations—and how these interactions link with the patient's story.

Wilson (1996) compared therapy with jazz musicians making music together: "with words and actions . . . stories and metaphors all become part of the improvisational exchange" (p. 38). This same applies to an assessment interview, where the assessor is "like the jazz musician who listens to the phrases of the other player, copies them and then, in time, makes those phrases his own" (p. 37). There are certain rules that musicians play by; it is also the assessor's skill in the musical exchange of words and listening that enables new possibilities to emerge through interactive improvization.

Opening stories

The assessment process has begun long before "the two strangers" (Coltart, 1983) meet in the consulting-room. The patient has often given the matter considerable thought and can give reasons for his decision to seek help, or the need for psychotherapy has been diagnosed by a concerned other. An agency has been chosen, and action has been taken either by making a self-referral or by being referred by a third party.

For the assessor, the work—the thinking on one's feet, and the decision-making process—starts when she picks up the telephone to offer an appointment. She is alert and begins to listen and ask silent questions. What is going on in this person's life? What is the nature of the psychic pain? Is it an acute crisis or a chronic conflict flaring up? What has triggered action now?

That first encounter can be, and often is, a very straightforward one, simply making the practical arrangements to meet. Even then, the two voices and the words, exchanging the necessary factual information, begin to live and communicate on an unconscious level, with associations and memories. The two-way process of being both assessors and assessed has started, as well as the transference–countertransference projections.

By using vignettes from assessment consultations, we can see a way of listening to a patient's story and formulating his basic predicament. The story is looked at as a pattern that repeats earlier ways of relating and gives information about psychic structure and internal object relationships. In the following examples, personal details are given as illustrating an interactional pattern and have general significance as a model, rather than as a case history of an individual person.

The two first clinical examples concentrate on the initial contact; the third example is described in more detail, including the assessment interview that followed.

FIRST EXCHANGE—ON THE TELEPHONE

I picked up the telephone and heard a woman's voice—educated, middle-class, English—wanting to make an appointment for an assessment interview. We made the arrangements to meet, and then the patient, out of the blue, in an aggressive tone, asked: "What is your accent?" I was totally unprepared for this question, from that voice. I replied automatically: "Perhaps we can explore the significance of my accent to you when we meet." This is not the first time I have been asked this question, often by someone who also has a foreign accent, but on this occasion the question came as a total surprise and left a feeling of intrusion.

I was utterly amazed at my strong reaction after I had put the telephone down. My countertransference response was full of anger; I felt invaded and exposed. The question, and the way in which it had been asked, fed into my prejudice that, after so long in this country, I can still be seen as a foreigner. The exchange that had taken place needed to be kept in my mind as an unconscious communication from the patient and as prologue to the assessment interview.

The patient arrived, and I was taken by surprise a second time. The image I had conjured up in my mind to match the voice proved to be utterly wrong. In front of me was a young black woman, British, born in this country, who said she did not know who she was.

Her childhood story was of a missing, black father, an abusive, white step-father, and a powerless, silenced black mother. This childhood world was now both her inner and outer reality. Her own face had become her enemy; the protective mother inside her was powerless. There was a raging fury and a wish to attack the intruders she felt surrounded by. The invasiveness I had felt made sense; she had spotted and identified "the stranger" in me, in my voice. By having had the telephone exchange, and acknowledging my countertransference response, we could explore her question: "What is your accent?" Behind the question lay her unconscious anxieties: "Are you able to hear my story, or is it going to be coloured by your prejudices and your accent?" "Can you bear to hear my pain?"

THE CONCERNED FATHER'S DEPRESSED SON

How does the assessor react if someone telephones to make an appointment on behalf of someone else? This usually indicates that behind the patient there is an emotionally involved and concerned other, who has an investment in the psychotherapy assessment. It is clear that they have already made their own assessment about who the disturbed one is in the relationship. What implications does this communication have for the referred patient's suitability for psychotherapy?

A father telephoned asking to make an appointment for his son. He told me that his son was depressed and was in need of psychotherapy. Before making any decisions, I asked the age of the son; he was 24. I noted that this father held onto his parental role and had a need to take responsibility for his adult son. I asked myself: was the father, by referring his son, asking for help himself? What did the son's depression communicate to the father? Did he want to relinquish his responsibility, hand it over to a professional "parent"?

I asked the father to consider what would help his son most—continuing to take action on his son's behalf, or encouraging him to be responsible for himself? Also, as he was so concerned for his son, would it be useful, in the first instance, for them to be seen together? On the other hand, would he prefer to support his adult son's independence by leaving him to take action in his own right? By giving options, I was handing back the decision-making to the father, hinting that there might be a shared problem—a failure to differentiate—between father and son. It also indicated that the father had a choice in the role he could take vis-à-vis his adult son. I suggested that father and son clarify between them what they see as the most appropriate way forward, and then contact me again. The son telephoned later that same day to make his own appointment. Perhaps in the transference I had already become a father, encouraging separation of the father–son couple?

This prologue could be seen to illustrate the son's core dilemma; the interactive pattern, the failure to differentiate between the external father and the adult young man, might reflect the structure of the son's inner object relationships. How to say "farewell to childhood" and move on might be a central theme.

The subsequent assessment interview confirmed my hypothesis. The son—in his attempt to separate from his parents—had formed a relationship with a young woman in which he took the parental, protective role. She saw his care as a temporary crutch and a stepping-stone in her move towards independence and self-sufficiency. He felt used and let down by her, angry and envious of her success in the adult world. He became depressed.

The father stepped in as a protector, suggesting that the son returned home to be cared for and to recover. The young man felt a failure in his own eyes, and he felt he had let his good, caring parents down. He was attacking himself and had guilt feelings about the repressed "unjustified" anger towards his father, who had "rescued" him.

The son's symptom contained his conflict. The hero had made a U-turn, the angry energy had been turned inwards, and his fear of failure had immobilized him. Neumann (1954) looked on the image of the hero as a metaphor, symbolizing the conflicts of growing up. He saw the hero's first struggle in the separation from the mother and from the protective parental care. The father—in being a protective mother rather than an encouraging father—had made the son passive, reduced his activity, and pushed him back into dependency. For the son to realize his masculine potential, he needs to separate from the father, rather than merging with him as a defence against his unconscious wish to destroy/dethrone him. The envy that the patient felt towards his girlfriend contained his desire to achieve self-sufficiency. He needed both an external and internal separation from the depressing parents. The son transferred onto me his hope for help in becoming an adult. He needed to abandon his external parents and trust that they could survive without a child to protect.

"TRUST ME TO GET IT WRONG"

The referral—the prologue. In this case illustration, the wife acted as the initiator of the referral. By her action she indicated that she was actively involved in getting help for her husband, Mr S. The decision that needed to be made, there and then, was, should the assessor accept this third-party referral on the patient's behalf, or should the initial appointment be offered to the couple? The telephone call from the concerned wife was a sign that the referred patient's problem had affected the marital relationship.

The wife explained, in answer to my question why she and not her husband was contacting me, that she had agreed to make the practical arrangements as it was difficult for him to do so from his office. She was worried for him, he needed help, their marriage was all right. Her husband's father had died a few months ago, Mr S could not get over it, and he was still preoccupied with the death and the loss. I suggested her husband should contact me to make his own appointment. I wanted to test Mr S's own motivation.

The opening lines of Mr S's story, as told by his wife, were these. The death of his father, which had occurred a few months previously, had affected his equilibrium to a degree that had caused concern and had unbalanced the marital relationship. Why is there a need for outside help now? What is the wife communicating in wanting her husband "to get over it"? Her action in contacting the BAP indicated that she had made her assessment: the death of the father had a deep significance for her husband, and he needed professional help. I wondered, as the crisis was over, if her patience was running out? She needed her husband back, and a return to normal family life. She did not want to mother the lost, bereft little boy any longer. The dead father had taken her husband away from her; was she feeling excluded? How would a therapeutic relationship, from which she would be excluded, affect their marriage?

Mr S telephoned and reiterated what his wife had said: "My father died nine months ago; I do not know how to get over it." We made the usual practical arrangements to meet. Shortly before our appointment time Mr S telephoned a second time. He had lost his instructions for how to get to my consulting-room. I repeated them, and mentioned again that my consulting-room is an annex building to the house, and that it has a separate entrance. Mr S duly arrived, at the wrong door. Realizing his error, he said: "Trust me to get it wrong." I associated his comment with a parent–child interaction, a lost, anxious little boy being ticked off by an internal parental voice: "Trust YOU to get it wrong." I also noted my countertransference feelings of wanting to take care of the frightened little boy, despite the fact that in front of me was a tall man, perhaps in his late 30s, with a commanding presence, perfectly capable of getting it right.

In an article in the *Observer*, Adam Phillips (1996) makes a comment about self-imposed hide-and-seek: "The way we defend ourselves tells us, in disguised form, what it is we desire." Perhaps the patient was giving me two communications: "Trust me" and (he) "gets it wrong". Is it you or me, or is it the interaction between the critical parent and the anxious child, that gets it wrong? I had become part of his story, a parental transference figure. He needed to defend himself against reproach. The game of hide-and-seek had begun.

The assessment interview. The areas to be explored by the assessor for the decision-making on the person's suitability for psychotherapy would include:

- current life situation (work, close relationships, social network etc.);
- ego strength;
- whether the appropriate life tasks for the person's stage in his life cycle have been achieved (dependency/self sufficiency, work, marriage, parenthood);
- areas of conflict and tension;
- habitual defences used, problem-solving patterns or repeating patterns;
- background personal and family history;
- assessment of psychological-mindedness (Coltart, 1983);
- previous help sought.

In this story of the assessment interview with Mr S, I shall begin by sharing the manifest content, the factual information, as told by him, then explore his story, noting the underlying structures and the repeating interactional patterns, and consider how these patterns can be linked to his early childhood experiences and object relations and the adjustments and defences that have become part of the adult psychic structure. In considering the question "Why is help sought now?", we need to explore the time and space connections of the recent events. What is the communicative meaning of the structure breaking down? Could "Trust me to get it wrong" be listened to as the patient's unconscious communication, as a first dream, which, according to Jung (1945/ 1948), gives both the problem and its solution? "The dream is a spontaneous self-portrayal, in symbolic form, of the actual situation in the unconscious." Can the games of hide-and-seek be reframed, enabling Mr S to move on?

The prologue has given the assessor the patient's answers to the questions of what had brought him here and why now. His reason is his father's death and the disturbing effect that it has had. The timing of the referral is linked with "I should have got over it but I cannot do it" ("Trust me to get it wrong").

The actions before the interview and the brief meeting we had outside my consulting-room have given an indication of Mr S's feelings of anxiety, and of an internal critical parental figure, already transferred as a projection onto me. On the reality level, I am conscious that, for Mr S, admitting that he needs help is embarrassing and shameful, and that coming to talk to a stranger about the death of his father is difficult and painful. The first task is to make Mr S feel secure in the therapeutic space.

Once safely settled into his seat in the consulting-room, Mr S's opening comment is: "I have never thought that I might need psychotherapy. My wife insisted I seek help. My father is like an obsession in my mind. Why can I not put him to rest? What is wrong with me? My father is haunting me in my dreams, I see him coming up from his grave. We have nightly battles."

The death of the father.   The father, aged 62, had died suddenly, nine months ago, of a heart attack. He just collapsed in a public place. There was nothing anyone could do, he was dead before the doctor arrived. The father had had a warning a couple of years earlier and had been told to ease off; he had ignored the medical advice. His refusal to accept his heart condition and to take care of himself had made Mr S feel impotent and angry, particularly as there was a precedent: Mr S's grandfather had died, at the same age, in very similar circumstances, of a heart attack. Mr S could remember the shock well; he was 10 years old when it happened.

Mr S described his father as a perfectionist, emotionally detached and self-contained. The father demanded high achievements of himself and would not accept weakness. He had the same attitude towards Mr S. He never praised his son, was critical of him, and could not tolerate mistakes. Mr S felt that, even though he had had a successful career and had reached a high position in his line of business, his achievements had never been good enough for his father. Mr S's work had taken him and his family abroad for a period; the father had not come to visit them and had not seen his grandson. Mr S had felt deeply hurt and angry with his father but had not had the courage to challenge him openly.

The sudden death was an utter shock for the whole family. The first few months after the father's death had been busy, sorting out practical problems. He and his brother had spent a lot of time with their mother, helping her to cope. The legal and financial sides were now cleared, and his help was no longer needed. His younger brother had been able to step in and was running the father's company with the mother. They seemed to be over the death and were getting on with their lives.

Personal and family history. Mr S was the first-born, the older of two brothers; the younger brother was born fifteen months later. Mr S remembers him as having always been close to the mother and being a weak little boy, often ill, and not very successful at school, and the father took little interest in him. The brother is now seen by Mr S as a relaxed, happy person. He is married and lives close to his mother.

Mr S was never close to his brother as a child. Mr S was the strong, independent child. The only time that his mother showed concern for him was if he was ill. He was successful academically and good at competitive sports. His father, a feared and admired figure, demanded high achievements but never gave praise or showed approval.

Current life situation. Mr S married a warm, caring woman twelve years ago. For many years they enjoyed their couple relationship, both getting on with their careers. Two years ago their first child was born, which meant a major change in their relationship. His wife gave up her career to stay at home with their son. She is a devoted mother. Mr S feels that he has not had time to adjust to being a father and to learn to know his son; he often feels left out when he watches his wife and son together. His career has taken him away from home more frequently than before, which he resents, but he cannot change this as refusing to travel would sabotage his career. For the past nine months he has been over-involved with his father's death, first in sorting out the practical problems, and now his obsessional thoughts and his nightly battles are giving him no space and are terrifying him. His wife is worried and fed up.

Interactional patterns—internal and external object relationship. The key figures in the story are: a dead father and an adult son; an internal father who is not dead and a frightened son, who is battling in his dreams with his father's ghost.

Why is this successful man still tied, in his mind, to this father whom he could never please? Is he afraid that he might be heading towards the same fate as his father and grandfather, and die of a heart attack? Are the obsessional thoughts the vicious circle, keeping him safe from the breakdown of his inner, defensive psychic structure?

Could it be that the battle that was not fought with the living father now needs to be fought with the dead one? Are the nightly battles both his fear and his longing to join the dead father? Or is the battle caused by his desire to be freed from being tied to his father and his fear of separation from this ever-present, critical father? How can he be released to be his own man and his son's father? Can he trust himself to get it right?

There are also the external interactions, after the father's death, between the mother and two brothers. Both brothers step in as rescuers and protectors of the mother. The younger brother stays with the mother, and he takes over the empty place left by the father. Have the current events triggered a memory of an earlier loss of the mother to a rival brother? Are the nightly battles also envious attacks of the ghost from the past?

The age gap between the two brothers is only fifteen months. One could speculate that the arrival of an invader was experienced by Mr S as a shattering rejection by his mother. The loss of the good, safe mother came as a sudden shock, which had to be managed by defending against that loss. In his work on early infancy, Fordham (1978) stated that defences that are built up at too early an age tend to become pathological. "Trust me to get it wrong" could be seen as having roots in an experience of the infant not being heard or understood. The critical attacking other became part of the defence against the loss of the good mother. This inner-object relationship pattern is then re-experienced and confirmed in the relationship between Mr S and the detached, critical father. The critical father became an inner driving force, helping Mr S to excel in school and to move onto a successful career to gain the father's love and approval.

Time and space connections—why now? It is possible that the coincidences of events in space and time mean something more than mere chance. The death of Mr S's father was significant on several accounts. The grandfather and the father were both first-born sons in their families. They both died suddenly of a heart attack, at the age of 62, in similar circumstances. The death of the father became thus far more meaningful to Mr S, the first-born, than to the brother. Another coincidence was the fact that Mr S had only recently become a father and his son was fifteen months old when the grandfather died. The timing of these two events triggered subjective memories of an earlier loss of the mother when he was fifteen months old. With the birth of his son, Mr S has lost the exclusive relationship he had with his wife. At the same time his job had become more demanding, taking him away from his home. His brother joining the mother, after the death of the father, feeds into unresolved feelings of envy. The ego defences break down; the battle with the dead father has opened up a deep inner void.

Reviewing the communicative meaning of the opening stories

Returning to the three case illustrations, each patient came with an inner conflict they could not solve, causing pain and anxiety, and motivating them to seek professional psychotherapeutic help. An assessment of the perceived outcome of the consultation had already been made by the patient or by an other.

FIRST EXCHANGE—ON THE TELEPHONE

"What is your accent?", the opening question from the patient, was the first clue to this assessment. It was translated in my mind: "Can you be trusted to understand me and my conflicts?" "What will your accent be?"

The manifest problem presented by the patient was: "I do not know what I am." Her black face and her middle-class English voice did not go together. They isolated and separated her in her external relationships. She could not hide her face and had learnt to use her voice to spot the "stranger" in the other.

The external reality was mirrored in her internal object relationships. Her black mother—not born in this country—could not give the patient an identity; the internal, missing, black father was replaced by an external, abusive, white father. He had the power and knew the right language.

Gordon (1993), in discussing psychoanalysis and racism, states:

It is increasingly common now to try to understand racism in terms of Kleinian meta-psychology and it is true that Kleinian concepts appear particularly relevant to an understanding of racism, given the nature of racist discourse: envy of the mothering capacities of the black woman and the imputed sexuality of the black man and the black woman. [p. 69]

Could it be that the white stepfather had projected his envy of his black sexual rival onto the black man's child? The patient had joined the white aggressor, had taken his voice, but had lost her soul. The patient's view of herself became confused with how she was viewed by the other. The powerful, intrusive white stepfather cut the connection between the silenced mother and her child.

Can individual psychotherapy help this patient separate what is the collective evil in a society dominated by the white man's language from her personal search for her lost identity?

THE CONCERNED FATHER'S DEPRESSED SON

In referring his adult son, the concerned father indicated their joint difficulty of differentiation. The initial clarification by the assessor of what was the son's task allowed the son to take responsibility for his own life.

The separation anxieties between parent and child, communicated by the referral, were confirmed by the patient's story. He had failed with his adult task to leave home. He had made an attempt to say "farewell to childhood" and had moved to live with his girlfriend. In that relationship he became the caring/controlling mother/father figure. His girlfriend—unlike him—used the parental care that she received as a short-term crutch and moved on to adulthood and independence. The patient was unable to cope with the abandonment, the anger, and the envy.

He returned home to his parents. By that act he felt a failure in his own eyes as well as in his parents' eyes. The need to return home could also be seen as an attempt to re-establish his relationship with his parents as an adult. The father, acting as the referrer, might be asking for a detached other to step in and help them in their dilemma. The caring parents need to be abandoned for the hero's quest to continue. The therapist's task would be the setting up of an adult-to-adult contract with the patient and separating what therapy can and cannot be used for in his life task of saying goodbye to childhood.

"TRUST ME TO GET IT WRONG"

The sudden death of the father of this successful man, and the fact that "he cannot get over it", was the reason for referral. The external event had opened up an inner insecurity and had caused a collapse of the psychic defence structure.

In making my psychodynamic formulations, the critical father/ anxious child was identified as the core object relationship. The inner battle "Trust me to get it wrong" was seen as a defence against an earlier loss—the loss of a good mother. This loss had been experienced at the arrival of the younger brother when Mr S was fifteen months old. The sudden, abrupt, and premature separation had meant that the differentiation–individuation process was not completed on the infantile level, causing an internal split. The father's sudden death coincided with Mr S becoming a father, his son being fifteen months old when the father died. The birth of the son was a major change in his external life and had affected his relationship with his wife. In addition, in his work he was forced to do more trips abroad, leaving less time to be with his wife and son. He felt excluded. Thirdly, the original scene was repeated by the younger brother taking the father's place in the family business, triggering feelings of an earlier loss.

The nightly battles with his father's ghost could be seen as the delayed fights of an adolescent with a powerful father, fights that needed to be won for Mr S to be individuated to be his own internal father and to become a more available father to his own son. The nightly battles could also be seen as fear of a sudden death: the fear that he—as the first-born son—would be compelled to follow his father and grandfather.

In the assessment process, Mr S projected onto me both the critical father and the lost mother to whom he wanted to attach himself. A major restructuring of his inner resources would be needed, as well as the separation of his external reality—where he can be a good father and he is not his son's rival—from his inner reality. In the therapeutic space, the therapist and Mr S can create—as two adults—the inevitable hide-and-seek games of "who gets it wrong" and the battles between the critical father and the anxious child. Gradually, "Trust me to get it right" becomes a shared experience, allowing the healing of the inner split.

The ending

The ending of an assessment interview is an opening of a new story. In that meeting of the two strangers, and through the interactions that have taken place, the old story has been re-framed and transformed. Through the process of storytelling, listening, thinking, and formulating, a new reading can be shared, in which the psychic pain can be given a healing meaning.

CHAPTER SIX

The assessment consultation

Aslan Mordecai and Danuta Waydenfeld

"No man can reveal to you aught but that which lies half
asleep in the dawning of your knowledge"

Kahlil Gibran, *The Prophet*

The purpose of the assessment session is simple. It is not
to diagnose the prospective patient's condition nor his
psychopathology. It is merely to assess his suitability for
psychoanalytic psychotherapy (Tyson & Sandler, 1971).

The assessment session is in most cases the first encounter that
the potential patient has with psychotherapy. It is thus a bilateral
assessment. There is in one chair the therapist endeavouring to
find out whether the stranger in front of her is likely to benefit
from psychoanalytic psychotherapy: listening, looking, trying to
unravel the meaning of his words, of this person's story, observing his body language, absorbing all the messages and clues. The
person in the other chair does not know what to expect. He may
be anxious, even bewildered, probably unfamiliar with the process, but he too will be looking for clues in the scene that he is now

part of. He may be assessing the assessor, looking for signs and signals in her demeanour, her utterances, even in the room in which he finds himself, in order to get the impression as to whether this kind of therapy will meet his needs, will help him to deal with his emotional problems.

Starting the assessment

At this first encounter, the patient has to feel safe enough to trust the therapist and to begin to trust the process to which he may be committing himself. The assessor can help by making him feel comfortable and at ease. She must always, first and foremost, treat the patient with courtesy and respect, she must make him feel secure, heard, and understood. She ought to give him the impression that she is interested and accessible, not that she is placing herself in a position of authority in order to judge, dictate, or pronounce. An assessor who is, or is perceived as, cold, supercilious, or contemptuous does not make the patient feel that his needs are likely to be met. It is not unusual for a patient to relate a previous experience of assessment from which he had either walked out or not followed through. It may have been connected with the school of thought which advocates silence on the part of the assessor during the initial interview. But for most patients, especially for those with little knowledge of the therapist-as-blank-screen technique, this may be experienced as unnecessarily persecuting, rude, and even bizarre (Coltart, 1983). The naïve patient who has no experience of psychoanalytic abstinence feels lost, confused, and ignored, and his first impulse may be to flee.

One of the authors had a similar initial experience. He [A.M.] arrived for his assessment interview on time and was asked to go into the waiting-room. Having waited for half an hour past the appointed time, he was ushered into the consulting-room, where the assessor sat blankly and passively in total silence. After half an hour, during which the assessor did not utter a sound, she abruptly informed the, by now bewildered, would-be patient that the interview had come to an end, as there was no more time available to complete it; instead, the interview would be continued at another half-hour session a week later. At no point did the assessor offer an apology or explanation for the curtailed time, the inconvenience caused, or the discourteous behaviour.

The length of the assessment consultation is determined by the assessor and may vary with her experience, her speed of work, or the time available to her. It is useful, where possible, to make the session relatively open-ended, but with a time limit in mind. A number of practitioners try to leave a space of one and a half hours for an assessment interview as this allows for greater scope; however, there are reality limitations to the time that can be devoted, and an experienced assessor should be able to get all the information needed in the time available to her. This may require the skill of stemming the uncontrollable flow of words of certain very voluble patients and gently steering them into giving the necessary information.

The opening of the session can be quite simple. First, the therapist introduces herself, which in practice may take a form similar to the following:

> "My name is Rhoda Mapesbury, I am a psychoanalytic psychotherapist and also an assessor for the Clinical Service of the BAP. My job is to assess whether this form of therapy would be the one most helpful to you. If we both feel that it is so, and if you would like to go ahead, then I will try to find an appropriate therapist for you. . . ."

Some therapists also like to tell the patient at this opening stage that he will not be expected to make a decision at the end of the interview, that he may wish to have time and space to think it over before making a commitment to therapy. Other therapists like to leave this advice till the end of the session. It is, however, important not to rush into referring the patient after his possibly impulsive and later regretted decision to go ahead, as experience has taught us that this often leads to an abortive referral and to therapy sessions unnecessarily being kept open for an uncertain patient.

Taking the patient's history

The introduction may be followed by an open-ended invitation. "Tell me about yourself and why you are seeking therapy now" might be quite a useful, general-purpose opening gambit. It is an open-ended and unstructured encouragement for the patient to lead us where we can follow, in order to find out what factor precipitated the decision to enter therapy at this precise moment of his life, and how the patient sees himself as a person and in relation to other people and to his environment. A certain length of time may be allotted to these areas before moving on to the next stage, which may be the exploration of the patient's history. At this point, some patients may volunteer all the information about their family of origin, their parents, siblings, their own place in the family, the pattern of relationships, and so forth. Other patients may become reticent, feeling disloyal about revealing painful family secrets or unusual constellations. Some may show the first signs of possible resistance by sentences like, "I had a happy and uneventful childhood" or "I have no memory of my life before the age of 15".

As much as therapists dislike asking questions, the assessor may find it necessary to ask directly for information at this stage. In order to form a clear image of the person in front of us, we have to know about his early life, his relationships (loving, abusive, neglectful, etc.) within and outside the family, the age and other significant differences between the siblings, their respective genders, the personalities of the parents, the patterns of dominance and submission, the habitual ways of behaviour of the family as a whole and its individual members, the place of the family within the community. We want to hear about the school that he attended, his relationships with fellow students (friendships vs. isolation, being bullied or a bully, a leader or a follower) and teachers, and briefly something of his interests and attainments. We want to know how the person coped with the changes of adolescence, his emotional and sexual development, his sense and image of self. Was he docile or rebellious? What were his ambitions as opposed to those of his parents? Did he proceed to higher education? Next there is his transition to adult life: the chosen job or profession, relationships with other adults at work and leisure,

emotional and sexual relationships. We look at his partners, marriage or cohabitation, his relationships with his own children. We
may briefly enquire about the patient's health, his habits (including eating patterns and addictions), his use of drugs for medication
or recreation, his psychiatric history, if any, and whether he has
had any previous experience of therapy. Some assessors like to
take notes during the interview, others may prefer to give their
undivided attention to the patient.

Explaining analytic therapy to the patient

Now that the therapist has satisfied herself that the patient has
given as much relevant information as is possible, it is important to
go on to the next part of the assessment interview. This part of the
interview can be likened to an educative process: explaining and
helping the patient to see what may actually happen in therapy.
Ordinarily, it is useful to devote at least one-third of the interview
time to this section, which will be of significance to both the patient
and the assessor. It is about looking closely at the practical implications of psychoanalytic psychotherapy, so that the patient can truly
make up his mind whether this is the right treatment for him,
having explored issues such as the likely length of treatment, frequency of sessions, fees, the couch versus the chair, transference,
free association, dream analysis, holidays, and so forth (Bleger,
1967; Langs & Stone, 1980; Winnicott, 1955.)

We find it essential to go over all these issues with the patient,
as this is often one of the keys to a successful assessment interview.
People have all sorts of fantasies about what actually happens in
the psychoanalytic setting, frequently based on knowledge from
films, media, friends, and books. Sometimes there is a confusion
about the different terminology: what is the difference between a
psychologist, psychiatrist, psychotherapist, analytical psychologist, psychoanalyst, and counsellor? They might also want to know
what route people take in becoming a psychoanalytic psychotherapist. One can, of course, wonder analytically with the patient why
these terms are relevant: is one group better than the other? However, it is equally—if not more—important to provide the patient

with as many facts as possible, so that he can think clearly about the choice that he will have to make when he leaves the interview. It would be quite easy, but not altogether helpful, if one just ana- lysed his questions instead of giving appropriate answers to the practical ones. There will be enough time in the therapy to explore the hidden agenda in the patient's questions. It may be useful, however, to observe whether the patient can make use of certain interpretations in the interview, always bearing in mind that, as one has only been with him for a very short time, these interpreta- tions are likely to be no more than hypotheses at this early stage. (Perhaps it could be argued that interpretations are never more than hypotheses at any stage.)

One usually finds that the main task of this part of the assess- ment interview is to make it clear to the patient that psychoana- lytic psychotherapy is usually a long-term treatment. He may come to the interview with the assumption that long-term therapy lasts several weeks, or at the most months. Most patients are sur- prised when they discover that to consider therapy seriously they would have to think about seeing a psychotherapist for a mini- mum of a year, but more probably for two, three, or four years, maybe even more (Sandler, Dare, & Holder, 1973). There is a fine balance to be drawn at this stage of the interview: if the patient feels that therapy will be interminable, this may cause him too much anxiety and he may even not bother to consider it further; one must, however, be as clear as possible, so that the patient can ultimately make an informed choice (Freud, 1913c).

There are ways of reducing some of the anxiety caused by mentioning the length of treatment. Certainly, explaining the rea- sons why it takes such a long time can put the matter into perspective, thus diminishing some trepidation. One can begin by pointing out that however much one might have a conscious wish and intention to change, to look at, and to explore certain parts of one's life, one has an equally powerful—if not more powerful— unconscious wish not to change, not to look, not to explore. It is as if there is one part of the patient requesting help and wanting to change and another hidden part sending out signals saying, *I don't want to change!* Usually patients can readily accept and under- stand this struggle and conflict within themselves. They seem to be able to relate to this form of resistance and can appreciate that this can be a major reason why therapy takes such a long time. These issues can be expressed in a variety of ways, such as coming late for appointments, not turning up at all, forgetting dreams, remaining silent for several sessions or, on the contrary, not letting the therapist speak at all, forgetting payment of fees, and so on.

The assessor has to explain that so much of psychoanalytic psychotherapy is about making the unconscious, conscious. Only then is it really possible to deal with areas in one's life that have been hidden up to now. Whilst the material is deep down and unconscious, it is very difficult to come to terms with it, knowing only that "something" inside is affecting one's external life. It is *the internal life* that one is seeking to bring to the surface in order to do something about it. But it can take a long time to bring this inner life to the conscious realm (Coltart, 1988). We find the metaphor of an archaeological dig useful to help the patient understand that therapy is a slow, painstaking process (Freud, 1913c). There are some other useful metaphors, which are described later.

The therapist can point out resistance in a patient if she feels that it could be useful. For instance, there is the example of the patient who came very late—in fact, halfway through his appointed assessment time. It transpired that he had left home in a rush, discovered that he was out of petrol, and had to go to a garage to fill up in order to get to his assessment consultation. When he got to the garage he then found that he had left his wallet at home; so he had to rush back, get his wallet, fill up, and then race to the session. Much of the initial assessment was then used to work out why he was so ambivalent about getting help. In fact, because the incident was looked at in such depth, he was able to consider seriously whether psychoanalytic psychotherapy was what he really wanted. He was able to use the insights he gained during the interview, and he has gone on to have a very successful therapy. Putting himself under unnecessary stress by coming late, setting himself up to fail, and not wanting to pay are intimately combined in this illustration.

After the assessor has tried to convey the reality that psychoanalytic psychotherapy is usually a long-term commitment, primarily because there are so many defences that have to be worked through, the patient needs to know about the intensity of treatment. He should know at this stage that the type of therapist he would be referred to would have been trained to see patients three or more times a week, but that it would be possible to refer him to a therapist who would agree to see him once or twice a week. However, the patient does need to know that the different frequencies would make a considerable difference to the type of therapeutic experience that he might eventually have. Seeing someone once a week is more likely to mean working on issues on a more superficial level than when going more frequently. Often, patients who opt for once-weekly sessions may be afraid of going too deeply and too quickly into areas of their life that they have kept hidden from themselves. Also, it can be used defensively, insofar as they may feel that they cannot possibly speak about a certain topic, or open up emotionally, if they know that they are not going to see their therapist again for another week.

Patients are encouraged to consider seeing the therapist at least twice weekly; there is more of a flow between sessions, it is not so much on the surface, and there is less chance of defences building up between sessions. The more frequently they go to sessions, the more likely they will encounter and experience feelings that would be difficult to face if they only went once weekly (Quinodoz, 1992). However, many patients come to the assessment interview expecting to see a therapist not more than once a week for maybe six months at the most, so it is quite an adjustment in their thinking to consider seeing someone more intensively and for a long time. It is explained that they may wish to increase the frequency of their sessions as time goes on, though they may not feel ready for it at present. It is not uncommon for psychotherapists to have patients who have started therapy once weekly and who have within a couple of months gradually increased the frequency of sessions (Shapiro, 1984).

Sometimes there is, of course, a practical reason why patients would not consider having therapy more than once a week. There was a time, until perhaps fairly recently, when analytic patients were recruited from well-to-do middle classes and the so-called intelligentsia, and daily sessions were easily fitted into their timetables and their budgets. Lately, the "talking cures" have become the subject of various media presentations (films, popular books, articles etc.), "therapy" has become part of the average person's vocabulary, and the base from which patients come to us has been broadened to include people living on limited budgets, such as young people at the start of their careers, young married people with children and mortgages, and people in not very highly paid occupations. Their reality makes it possible to see a therapist only once a week, even though ideally they might be helped by more frequent sessions.

The patient has to give serious thought to his finances and has to recognize that therapy is going to be a major financial commitment for some years ahead. He may wish to see a therapist three, four, or even five times a week, and in some cases it is abundantly clear that it would have been an advantage. But if he does not have the financial resources, then it is more important for him to be in touch with the reality of his life and to go less frequently to start with, always hoping to increase his sessions when circumstances allow. The assessment interview provides him with a much-needed opportunity to think about his financial commitment and all the issues surrounding it, without the added pressure of having to decide immediately whether to go into therapy.

The patient should be informed of the fee for the assessment at the time of making the appointment. Should, however, the question of payment for the assessment arise during this initial telephone call or later in the interview, it has to be dealt with in a straightforward and businesslike manner. If the patient queries the amount and tells the assessor of his financial difficulties, his present lack of employment, or some other strained circumstances causing him difficulty in paying the one-off assessment fee, it may be appropriate to discuss briefly at this point the general cost of therapy and possibly suggest alternative options, such as treatment on the NHS, voluntary bodies, and so forth, or, if the patient is deemed a suitable candidate, the BAP Reduced Fee Scheme, which may be available to suitable patients for therapists in training. In certain cases, we may suggest individual or couples counselling, family therapy, or group therapy and, if possible, offer help in finding the right organization.

Some patients may use the whole issue of finances to run away from having intensive treatment. One has to be able to explore this aspect of their decision-making. Sometimes, even though they can actually afford to see a therapist at least three times a week, they are unwilling to make therapy such a high priority, perhaps because they feel that they do not deserve it, that it would be an indulgence; alternatively, they may prefer to spend their money in other ways that they may value more highly. Clearly, they have to spend time reflecting on what they really want out of therapy, and how much they are prepared to put in, not only financially but also in other ways. Thus, therapy is no different to so many other situations: you only get out of it what you put in—no more, no less.

Another issue that needs to be addressed at the initial assessment interview is the times of sessions. Some patients can be flexible about the times when they can see their therapist, whereas others cannot attend during the working day. Some are afraid that if the boss knows that they are seeing a psychotherapist, their career may be affected. Clearly, the patient needs to be able to decide whether, on a long-term basis, he can manage to attend during the day or not, and also how frequently. It often becomes clear to him that as he wants more sessions he can actually spare the time, and he may discover that he is not really concerned with other people's opinions. At the initial interview he is encouraged to think flexibly about his choices and the options open to him.

Going into details of therapy

Once the assessor feels reasonably sure that the patient has largely absorbed the practical implications of psychoanalytic psychotherapy, then it is time to try to look at some of the details of what he will face during treatment. There are some therapists who may frown on the suggestion that the patient needs to be educated into psychoanalytic psychotherapy. Greenson (1967), however, states quite clearly that we cannot demean a patient by imposing rules and regulations upon him without explanation and then expect him to work with us as an adult. If we treat him as a child by presenting him with our imperious and arbitrary attitudes and expectations, he will remain fixated to some form of infantile neurotic transference reaction. Greenson goes on to say that we should show consistent concern for the rights of the patient and the pain that the analytic situation imposes on him. Aloofness, authoritarianism, coldness, and rigidity do not belong to the analytic situation.

The patient is told that almost certainly he will be expected to lie on the couch and that his therapist will sit behind him. He will be asked to say whatever comes into his mind, however irrelevant or insignificant it may seem. He must try not to censor any information, whether felt by him to be good or bad, embarrassing, or humiliating. It may be a sexual fantasy or a dream; there may be thoughts about someone in his past, someone in his present—a partner, a colleague, the therapist. He must try to be as honest as possible, as it is through free association, dream analysis, and the transference relationship with his therapist that he can reach his unconscious. It is understandable that patients will often find free association difficult, especially if they have spent a lifetime trying to cover up what they really think and what they have never dared to verbalize (Modell, 1988).

Some patients can get very anxious at this stage, when they hear that not only are they expected to be open and truthful, but that they will also have to lie on the couch, thus feeling totally exposed, vulnerable, and infantile. One has to explain that the use of the couch allows one to focus on the internal world without the inhibition of facing the therapist all the time, when too much reality may interfere with the free expression of thoughts: the therapist's perceived facial expression, eye contact, movements whilst seated, and so forth may all give unnecessary messages to the patient. Furthermore, the point of psychoanalytic psychotherapy is to explore the inner world of the patient, and the less impingement from the therapist he encounters, the more he will be able to get on with the work in hand. Lying on the couch encourages the image of the therapist as a blank screen, so that the patient can project and transfer as much as possible onto it. This is much more difficult when constantly looking at the therapist (Temperley, 1984).

A patient of mine [A.M.] was obsessed with a fantasy that I had spent years of training as a psychoanalytic psychotherapist in order to get her onto the couch and rape her. This fantasy helps one understand the anxiety that a lot of patients have about lying down on the couch. They are afraid that they will be totally exposed, vulnerable, and quite helpless. They may feel like passive victims who will be unable to stop the physical, verbal, and auditory intrusions of the therapist. They will have succumbed completely. Furthermore, any dependence that they may experience on their therapist is exaggerated even more by the lying down on the couch, feeling infantile. Thus, for some patients, it is quite a difficult concept to grasp, and they need time and understanding to incorporate it into their thinking and expectations. They are reassured, though, if they know that some therapists may be flexible about the use of the couch if they feel that it is too disturbing for the patient at the beginning. Also, it is common for some therapists to allow patients to use the chair if they see them only once a week.

Having explained the concept of free association, the inner world and the couch, the concept of transference should also be dealt with in the assessment interview, albeit briefly. Patients will often ask about the difference between psychoanalytic psychotherapy and counselling. Apart from the length of treatment and the frequency of sessions, it is useful to give them some idea of the transference. One can show them that not only will the therapist be concerned with the relationships that the patient has on the outside, but she will also look at the relationship that the patient has on the inside—that is, with the therapist in the consulting-room. One explains that the patient may see the therapist in different roles: as a cold father or an overprotective mother, a harsh teacher or an unforgiving friend, just to give a few examples. These are attributes that belong to the patient's past, which are projected or transferred onto the therapist, and can give the therapist clues as to how the patient perceives and deals with people in his life.

One woman spent a good part of the initial consultation trying to get me [A.M.] to make an immediate decision for her— whether she should move to another city. When I pointed out that I could not really be expected to make the decision for her, she became upset and eventually started to cry. I gently made an interpretation that it was possible that she was seeing me as the strict and unyielding father whom she had earlier told me she had. The transference interpretation seemed to help her. She reflected on what I said, stopped crying, and proceeded to tell me how she often sees partners as cold, uncaring, and unresponsive and then has to end the relationships. We wondered together how much she may project into them what belongs to her relationship with her father.

It is mainly through working through these projections/transferences that the patient can understand what has been going on in his inner life.

Another route to the unconscious is through the analysis of dreams. It is a good way of discovering how much the patient is in touch with his unconscious, how much he is willing to open up and explore areas of his life that often are hidden from his conscious, rational mind. He is encouraged to try to remember his dreams if he decides to go ahead. Resistance to therapy can sometimes be shown by the paucity of dreams that are brought to the sessions. The reverse is sometimes true as well. Resistance can be apparent when a patient floods the sessions with dreams.

Payment for missed sessions and the length and frequency of holidays also have to be taken into account. Patients need to be told that normally they have to pay if they miss sessions, as that time is reserved for them. Different therapists may have slightly different ways of working with the external structures, and patients are encouraged to explore these aspects at the first interview with the therapist to whom they are referred. In the assessment interview, however, they are told what the generally accepted practices are. They are told that therapists take holidays, that the breaks will differ slightly between therapists, and that the patient will be informed of them in advance. Breaks usually consist of about four weeks in the summer, two weeks at Christmas, and two weeks at Easter. Patients may be expected to pay for sessions if they take their holidays at times differing from those of the therapist, especially if the therapist takes long breaks. Taking holidays at these different times is also inadvisable, as it interrupts the continuity of the treatment. It is important for patients to have as much information about the external structures as early as possible, partly from the assessor and more fully from their therapist, to prevent later misunderstandings.

The assessor needs also to explore how receptive the patient will be to analytic interpretations. One can try to find appropriate material in the interview and then make an analytic interpretation to see how the patient is able to use it (Brown & Pedder, 1979).

This may give the assessor a clue as to how suitable the person is for psychoanalytic psychotherapy and whether he would be able to use the analytic sessions to his best advantage.

> For instance, a patient I [D.W.] once saw for assessment told me how he had saved his widowed mother from almost certain financial ruin through bad investments she had made. He temporarily gave up his career to concentrate on her financial welfare, and when he was sure he had turned her losses to profits, he went back to his career. Some years later, he started a relationship with an older woman, who began having financial difficulties in her business. So, he left his job and made a financial success of her business too! But he was very ambivalent about the relationship. He was not at all sure that he wanted to carry on with it. I suggested that he was angry and tired of always being the rescuer, always doing the parenting; he had habitually appeared strong, yet he felt very weak inside and was desperate to get help for himself. This interpretation seemed to hit home, and he was able to enlarge on it in the assessment interview, bringing up further examples of himself as the saviour of his family, and eventually was keen to be referred on.

The capacity for insight is important if the patient is to benefit from psychoanalytic psychotherapy. The assessor needs to know whether the patient is able to relate his present predicament to situations in the past, and whether he is able to see that there are definite patterns of behaviour that are constantly influencing his life. If so, then the assessor can conclude that he is probably capable of making links with the past, and of accepting the concept of repetitive, neurotic behaviour. However, if a patient tells you that he had a very happy childhood, that his present relationships are fine, that there is nothing wrong with his life, yet he cannot understand why everything feels so bleak, does it mean that he has no capacity for insight and will not benefit from therapy? Or does it mean that he has built up a very powerful defensive structure, which will need all the skill and patience of a therapist to dismantle? Ultimately, if the patient shows a great need and a willingness to go further into therapy, then it is essential to give him the benefit of the doubt and refer him on, especially if both he and his therapist are made aware of the possible strength of his resistances.

Recognizing and using the countertransference, and its effect on the patient, is also a good diagnostic tool, allowing one to see whether the patient could benefit from psychoanalytic psychotherapy.

A patient I [D.W.] once interviewed spent most of the session telling me at great length about all the qualifications she had (they were considerable) and all the important jobs and posts she had been appointed to (they were quite extraordinary). Yet, even though she was telling me how special she was and how satisfied she was with her life, I was filled with intolerable sadness. I just could not understand where this was coming from. I remember wondering if it had come from a session with my previous patient—or could it be from something in my personal life? But as the patient sitting opposite me was continuing to tell me how successful she was, this unutterable sadness was welling up in me, and I gently asked her if her success stories were covering up any unhappiness (Green, 1986). At this she just broke down and wept and was able to reveal all the real pain and problems that she had been hiding. The sadness that was my countertransference immediately left me, and I was able to help her begin to own and take responsibility for her pain (Limentani, 1972). Only then did it become feasible for her seriously to consider embarking on an analytic journey.

Nearer the end of the assessment interview, we may sometimes describe psychoanalytical psychotherapy in metaphors. Patients coming to psychotherapy for the first time can relate to it more easily this way. They can understand it being a journey and can get great comfort from seeing it as one that they share with another person. They have often felt alone for too long. Most patients also readily accept the idea of therapy being like a jigsaw puzzle (Freud, 1923c [1922]). They go to their therapist with a half-completed picture, but most of the bits do not fit, others are not in the right place, some have been forced together, and some are lost.

They can understand that it is the job of therapy to sort out the pieces and then put them together in the right place for the first time. Sometimes, one will know where the bits should go; at other times, it is unclear what they mean and where they would fit, and one has to wait until the picture becomes clearer. But, most important of all, the patient has to accept that there are no shortcuts, as neither he nor the therapist can be aware of what the finished picture will look like. So it is even more of a Herculean task to try to complete it. The metaphor of the archaeological dig, mentioned earlier, is also a useful one; one can compare the process of therapy to one of digging and discovering—and the deeper one digs, the more forgotten and hidden the structures that one uncovers.

Concluding the assessment

In the last part of the assessment interview, it is useful to find out about the patient's health. Many clues to it may already have been gathered. The patient may have complained of various symptoms, and it is a dangerous assumption on the part of the therapist to label them all as psychosomatic. There is the well-known apocryphal story of the therapist who kept interpreting her patient's recurring headaches and missed sessions as resistance, while the patient was developing a brain tumour from which he eventually died. I myself [A.M.] had a patient who complained of various ill-defined discomforts and newly developed impotence, which, in view of his history, could easily have been given valid interpretations. Erring on the side of caution, I suggested a visit to his GP, who in turn referred him to a specialist, and a diagnosis of diabetes was arrived at and confirmed by tests. On the other hand, if during the assessment we are presented with a jumble of disconnected, odd, or bizarre symptoms, we need to consider what kind of psychopathology is hiding behind the "physical" façade. In Freud's time, many such strange presentations were indicative of hysteria (Freud, 1896c). Today, for various reasons, hysterics come to us with rather different presenting symptoms, and one rarely sees a case of florid hysteria like Anna O. or Dora coming for assessment in private practice. Having talked of "symptoms", we have to stress, however, that making a diagnosis is not one of the assessor's tasks, and though some of us are medically qualified, the greater majority are not. The relevant criterion for all assessors is: will this patient be suitable for psychoanalytic psychotherapy? Or, putting it the other way round: is psychoanalytic psychotherapy the best choice of treatment for this patient?

A knowledge of the patient's psychiatric history is appropriate, and information about his use of drugs, psychotropic and recreational, might be elicited at this point. This, in turn, may bring us to addictions and to the question of whether someone with a serious addiction to drugs or to alcohol is ready for psychoanalytic psychotherapy, or whether he needs to deal with his addiction first. Many patients coming to us with depression as the presenting problem have, in the past, seen their GPs or psychiatrists and are regularly taking antidepressants. It is not the assessor's role to question the treatment, but she has to take note of it and pass this information, along with other relevant material, on to the therapist to whom she is referring the patient.

Before moving on to practical issues, one may ask the patient whether there was anything that he had omitted from his story or felt too uncomfortable to talk about. One may be quite surprised to hear so late in the session a hesitant admission of something that the patient felt reluctant to talk about: an illicit sexual relationship, sexual abuse, incest, or dishonest dealings or guilty concealments.

Now is the time for more practical concerns and for dealing with the patient's wishes. What transport will the patient use? Which geographical areas are accessible for him? The assessor will need to know whether the patient has any firm views—for example, whether he would like to be seen by a man or by a woman. More often than not, the patient does not mind one way or the other, and many therapists feel that it is not a relevant issue. Occasionally, though, the patient will admit to a preference, and we feel that it is important to find for him a therapist of the chosen sex. Clearly, there is an underlying need of his to see the therapist of a particular gender, either to work out past difficulties or because he feels that he will be more at ease with such a therapist. It does not seem reasonable to us to insist on referring the patient to a therapist whose gender is not his choice, especially if the patient had been asked.

If the patient is psychologically sophisticated, the assessor would ask whether he has a preference for a therapist of any particular school of thought. Interestingly enough, if a patient ever spontaneously requests a therapist of a particular orientation, almost invariably he will ask for a Jungian analyst. The usual fantasy is that the Jungian analyst is more interested in spiritual matters and dreams, art, and religion and is willing to be more flexible. The stereotype of the Freudian psychotherapist is of someone who is cold, arrogant, controlling, and obsessed with sex. Clearly, the assessor has to look more closely with the patient at these thoughts and ideas, and try and elucidate why he feels this way. Ultimately, though, he must be given his choice (Pollock, 1960).

It is, of course, not always possible to meet the patient's specifications. When he tells you: "I would like to see a male Jewish Jungian therapist, aged between 40 and 50, within walking distance of Barnet tube station, after 7 p.m., who charges not more than £20 per session", you have to question whether the patient is genuinely serious in his quest for therapy or whether he is ambivalent, or perhaps showing early signs of resistance. He may also be setting himself up for a situation in which he is not able to get help, thus confirming his existing fear that he is an irredeemable failure, beyond the reach of therapy. He may have fantasies about the ideal therapist, like a patient recently seen who, as a small child, had lost his father and who was looking for an idealized father–therapist, who, he was also convinced, could not possibly exist.

With the assessment interview now drawing to a close, it is helpful to inquire whether there are any further questions that the patient would like to ask. We feel that it is essential that the patient is allowed to ask whatever he wants at this interview, because so often a patient who goes for help is actively discouraged from asking anything and goes away frustrated and angry. It is important always to recognize that this is an assessment interview, not a therapy session in which the therapist may want to interpret questions rather than give answers. Patients are told that the assessment interview differs from an actual session in many ways, and that the response to questions is one of them. Of course, this does not mean that none of the patient's questions will be explored analytically in the assessment interview; it just means that he is more likely to get a straight answer. Some caring and humanity needs to prevail in such potentially stressful and anxiety-provoking situations.

One of the questions that the patient frequently asks is what happens if he cannot get on or does not like the therapist to whom he has been referred. We do try to explain—in terms accessible to an unsophisticated patient—the possibility of negative transference to the new therapist or the potential strong positive transference to the assessor. We do also reassure the patient, however, that we are prepared to give him another chance with a different therapist.

The allotted time is running out, and the assessor has by now formed a fairly accurate mental picture of the person assessed and has come to a conclusion as to his suitability. If he is deemed suitable, the therapist may reiterate her earlier explanation of the need for time for reflection before the patient commits himself to therapy.

There may be various reasons why the patient is considered not suitable for psychoanalytic psychotherapy. He may have a serious psychiatric condition requiring treatment in the more containing environment of an institution. A patient will not benefit from therapy unless he has a reasonable level of intelligence, though this must not be confused with education—I have seen bright patients with very basic education who made remarkable progress in therapy and actually went on to improve their educational and occupational status. Then there is the often quoted ability for "psychological thinking" (Coltart, 1992), without which the patient and therapist may feel that they are speaking a foreign and mutually incomprehensible language.

It is not always easy to tell the patient that our particular brand of therapy is not going to benefit him, and what could be felt by the person as rejection must be couched by us in the most acceptable terms, with advice at the same time as to alternative options. And, as stressed at the beginning, courtesy and consideration for the patient and for his feelings take precedence over any negative feeling or countertransference that the therapist may have formed in the course of the interview.

Finally, the patient is encouraged to go home and think about the interview, to reflect on all that he has discovered in the time that he has been with the assessor. He needs to consider carefully the three commitments that he will have to make—emotional, financial, and time—each inextricably linked to the other. He is told that he should feel free to contact the assessor when he has made up his mind, whether the moment he gets home, the next day, in two or three weeks, or even longer. He needs his own space, away from the assessment interview, to work out if this is what he really wants. The patient needs to feel that he is making an informed and free decision about entering therapy. He should feel under no pressure to give an answer immediately. He is also told that a therapist will normally be found within two weeks of him actually re-contacting the assessor, after he has made up his mind. Our policy is to try not to keep people in distress waiting. Much of the initial assessment interview is therefore to make sure that the patient feels listened to, is given a good idea about what he should expect, and is assured that we would try to find the most suitable psychoanalytic psychotherapist for him. We would also reassure him that we would be willing to refer him to another therapist should he feel, after the first few sessions, that he is not able to work with the therapist to whom he had been referred. His needs regarding times, fees, location, and sex of the therapist would certainly be taken into account.

The interview is now over. There are the BAP booklets that the patient may be offered that explain the process of therapy. The account is presented, and the assessment fee is paid. If there are sudden "hand-on-the-doorknob" outpourings, a second interview may be offered, though this is rarely necessary. We like to treat our patients as we ourselves would like to be treated; thus we say goodbye with courtesy and warmth.

CHAPTER SEVEN

Transference and countertransference in the assessment consultation

Mary Rosalind Stumpfl

"Bridge over troubled water"

Simon and Garfunkel

W here else but in an assessment interview do two strangers meet like this? With an agenda, spoken or unconscious, which asks that the prospective patient reveals, as much as he is able, his life and the hopes and fears of his inner world. He may come with trepidation at such a prospect, or with high hopes at the idea of meeting someone who will listen and understand. He has probably never been given space for such a purpose. Whether hopeful or anxious (often both), he will wonder about this person who is offering him time and attention. Is he an inquisitor, or a good and understanding parent? Will the assessor stand in critical judgement, or will he offer the hope of a Utopian "cure" for the troubles that have plagued the patient who ventures into this unknown space? And what do we, as assessors, expect and hope for? Perhaps our wish is for an articulate and intelligent person with the capacity to examine his responses to life and to mobilize his ego to make links between past and present. Is this sometimes wishful thinking? It is certainly not possible to empathize with every stranger who walks through the door. But we must keep an open mind, being especially vigilant about our personal, social, and cultural prejudices. If one can recognize and examine both transference and countertransference, there are truly very few who are not capable of "arousing human sympathy" (Freud, 1895d, p. 265), even though at the end of the interview the assessor may feel that psychoanalytic psychotherapy may not be the most appropriate form of help for him.

One's awareness of the patient's transference and of one's own countertransference should be seen as signposts along the road to understanding the patient's unconscious, and the importance of this should not be underestimated. Schubart (1989, p. 423) writes that a meeting of this kind " also includes the psychoanalyst with his highly individual reactions to the patient and the latter's verbal and non-verbal communications. It is an encounter between two people with different roles in, and contributions to, the staging and understanding of the unconscious scene"—that is, of the transference–countertransference relationship. Little (1951) states that "any analysis postulates both an analysand and an analyst, in a sense they are inseparable. And similarly transference and countertransference are inseparable". Furthermore, she says, "I think there is an attitude towards countertransference, i.e., towards one's feelings and ideas, that is really paranoid or phobic, especially where the feelings are or may be subjective". And so it must be said for all assessment consultations.

Greenson (1992) has emphasized the importance of the initial telephone call, which heralds the start of the transference and countertransference. Each of us, patient and assessor, is at that moment working in the dark, with only our fantasies to keep us company. If the prospective patient sounds curt, even rude, our own defensive countertransference responses must be carefully monitored. On the other hand, should the patient sound relaxed and friendly, arrangements flow with comparative ease. However, it is all too easy to allow oneself to be seduced into slipping out of an observing stance, thereby weakening a capacity to think. (For instance, in my own case, should such friendliness be combined with a North American accent similar to mine, I must be even more careful to be aware of my countertransference lest I be drawn into a collusive exchange with the patient.) One must keep a careful eye upon over-familiarity such as the immediate use of the assessor's first name or too-ready comments upon the decor of the consulting-room (bearing in mind that some of the latter may be valid in terms of comfort or discomfort and how it reflects the therapist's own self-image). Such familiarity may indicate a need to take control of the situation and not allow the assessor her expertise.

Upon meeting, I have often been told that "on the way here" the patient had an idea that he was floundering and unsure while I would be the "expert" who would "know everything". Of course, this is not always expressed directly but manifests itself in many ways, and the assessor must be careful that he does not enact the role projected upon him. Certainly the patient should experience the assessor as knowledgeable—but also approachable and willing to listen and to learn. It is of the utmost importance to facilitate, but neither to alarm nor to seduce.

History taking is, of course, essential, and here again there is a sensitive area to negotiate. Questions and comments may be experienced as intrusive. If a patient's ego capacities cannot be mobilized by the assessor, making links between past and present, our countertransference may lead us to feel frustrated, if not virtually useless. Sometimes we must accept that we cannot help the patient to open the door to self-examination and thus to constructive growth. In some such cases, it seems as though we have before us a recalcitrant child who needs to undermine the efforts of the adult to reach him and whose capacity for self-reflection has not developed past the paranoid–schizoid stage. Usually, the assessor finds that the countertransference has moved from a feeling of frustration to one of sadness that this patient is unlikely to benefit from psychoanalytic psychotherapy.

A woman in her 30s came for an assessment interview. She complained that she felt constricted in all aspects of her life and derived no satisfaction from her job nor from her present relationship with a man, which did indeed sound to be very limited, both emotionally and sexually. I experienced her as encased within a glass box through which she peered at me but did not reach me, nor I her. I felt she did not see me as a live, present person. She sat with her hands gripping the arm of the chair and spoke in what I took to be an English accent, but it sounded stilted and I could not place it. After a while I learned to my great surprise that she had been in this country for only eighteen months and that she had been born and brought up in a city in Canada not far from that in which I grew up. In such a short time, she had managed to shed her accent and adopt another, in the unconscious quest of finding a new identity. I mentioned, with hindsight somewhat ill-advisedly, where I came from. She seemed uninterested, and, unlike virtually every other patient I have seen who comes from North America, she did not comment upon my accent, which is fairly pronounced. Here, an instance of projective identification resulted in my own need to confirm my identity (you can take someone out of his country, but you cannot take his country out of him). Such a lack of curiosity as she displayed does not bode well for imaginative adventures into the psyche.

Searles (1973) comments that in this stage of ambivalent symbiosis in which ego boundaries are by definition unreliable in either participant, there is much of both projecting and introjecting, with each person feeling threatened by the other by reason of the other's personifying one's own as-yet-unintegratable inner contents.

I learned further that she had been brought up in a middle-class suburban area, the only child of originally working-class parents. Her experience was that their energies and interests were wedded to the culture of the community, which emphasized social status and economic advancement. Her task was to be like the neighbours, only better. I thought that she had been given no encouragement to grow and develop as an individual child and young adult.

It was difficult to know how she saw me, as there were so few clues. I wondered whether I was a parental figure who could not and would not acknowledge her needs, but none of my tentative and, I hope, careful explorations aroused even a glimmer of recognition of any links between then and now. I felt helpless but also concerned for this young woman, who could not venture into the space where her present bleak existence might meet with hope for change and growth. Usually, upon such realization, the countertransference changes and the assessor, knowing that he cannot refer the patient for psychoanalytic psychotherapy, feels sadness rather than frustration. I wanted to suggest alternative arrangements for her, but she did not contact me again.

As assessors we all come to an assessment interview carrying our own personal history of thoughts and beliefs: philosophical, socioeconomic, political, ethical. I hope that such views have been carefully thought out and that we can discern the difference between idealism and ideologism. It is extraordinarily difficult to feel compassion for a patient who presents himself, for example, as an extreme racist. How does one deal with this? Hopefully, one tries to look at the meaning of such a rigid stance and attempts to reach the ego that may be able to look at this defensive structure. This may not be possible. Coltart (1987, 1993) says that the "wish for recovery" is not the same as the "will to be analysed". I am certainly not suggesting that the Canadian patient described above was racist, only to suggest that her rigid defences precluded the "will to be analysed". Coltart suggests that one way of assessing this potential function indicating the will to be analysed is by temporarily going against the flow of the patient's thoughts and feelings at some well-judged dynamic moment.

A man verging on 60 came for an assessment. He was depressed and consequently had recently started to drink heavily. I sensed that he was very angry, and I was struck by his appearance, which was quite inappropriate for his age. He wore his hair in a ponytail, was dressed in tattered shorts, and had a conspicuous earring. Although these first impressions were not favourable for making a referral, he gave a clear account of his life and was able to make good links between past and present. These were interspersed with aggressive jibes at me, and in the countertransference I felt a need to control a defensive anger.

As a child he had difficulties in eating, so much so that his mother virtually force-fed him, to the point where he vomited, and on more than one occasion he was made to eat the vomit. After a few more angry responses to me, I began to feel like the force-feeding mother and, moreover, experienced the frustration this mother must have felt in having her food rejected. Finally, I said that I thought he was experiencing me in exactly that way, and then suggested that he was using his excessive alcohol intake as an attempt to take over the force-feeding himself and make himself sick. There was a silence, and then a broad grin spread over his face and he said: "I think you've got something there." Thereafter the interview was fruitful; we seemed to be two adults who could look at an angry and, in a sense, abused child and learn how this could influence the would-be adult. It is not always wise to voice the promptings of the countertransference, but occasionally, as in this case, it may prove mutative.

At the end of the session, he said "I wish I could come again at this time next week to continue talking with you." Where an assessment interview has been experienced as helpful, a patient may feel that he wants to stay with the assessor and not be passed on to another stranger, although it is made very clear at the beginning that this would be the procedure. Sometimes this impedes work with a therapist, perhaps even prevents it. In this particular case, thanks to the therapist's skills and to the patient's "will to be analysed", the transfer to his new therapist was fairly smooth, and he has made considerable progress.

I would add that a sense of humour, most importantly as evinced in an ability to laugh at oneself—as could this patient, following his recognition of his initial responses to me—is a most helpful signpost along the road to change and growth.

Two strangers have met and communicated, verbally and nonverbally. Each has assumed a role in the playing out of the transference and countertransference. Assessor and patient have worked—indeed, struggled—towards a place where they may find a bridge over which the patient may start his journey towards freedom from the psychic constraints by which he has been fettered. Sometimes the assessor may feel, at the end of the consultation, that the patient's journey may have started. But sometimes we have to accept that we could not dislodge the brakes that seem to have irrevocably immobilized movement.

But perhaps we have each learned something of our roles, in this meeting between two strangers.

CHAPTER EIGHT

Boundaries and difficulties in assessment

Philip Hewitt

"To mingle with the Universe, and feel
What I can ne'er express, yet cannot all conceal"

Byron, *Childe Harold*, C.IV, clxxvi

One of the stated aims of the British Association of Psycho-therapists is "to promote the practice of psychotherapy so as to bring it within reach of a wider section of the community"(*General Information Leaflet*). This ethical standpoint is reminiscent of another, which was expressed years ago by Dr Murray Jackson at the Maudsley Hospital, that every patient is entitled to a psychodynamic understanding of his situation, a view reinforced in his more recently published book with Paul Williams, *Unimaginable Storms* (1994). The search for meaning in psychosis is stressed as an attempt to help patients whose lives are threatened with meaninglessness save for a formidable armoury of clinical classifications and pharmacology. A dynamic under-standing of distress offers a kind of hope against untold levels of human despair, which may be converted into obdurate institutional resignation. This universal ethical principle is a motivating force and underlines the importance of the task of the consultant psychoanalytic psychotherapist to attempt, usually at one sitting, to give "an understanding" to a person who may have only just started to see himself as a patient and who by no means accepts himself as such.

What is meant by understanding is not a diagnosis or a prescription, but the reaching of a point of contact between therapist and patient, as well as an acknowledgement of inner and outer reality. Often, this may be only *a sense* between therapist and patient that something has occurred between them in the room, but this may be sufficient and preclude the need for further explanations at this stage. The principle of the "least said the better" usually operates in parallel with *a sense* of holding, which will not be conveyed by the unyielding and silent psychoanalytic consultant as so often caricatured. In fact, the therapist will be trying to address the anxieties that are identified in the couple (therapist–patient), putting some of it into words and continuing to think or hold on to other parts. It is a twofold skill that is learned and that also draws upon the capacities of each individual. It is the part of a process that is the beginning of some mutual acceptance of the human condition and a shared understanding between two people in a consulting-room. The therapist, unintrusive and thoughtful, is sensitive to links with the patient's past and present, conscious and unconscious life as it now happens in the room. The patient is given space to express himself and identify his needs, whilst the therapist tends towards abstemiousness and deference to the all-important first presentation of the patient.

The occasion has a curious and creative sense. It is a first and a last time; two almost complete strangers, one confiding and the other listening, thinking, linking, and responding. Both are there feelingly disposed to one another, emotional antennae acutely sensitized perhaps more in an animal way. The therapist carefully guards inner knowledge about the universality of unconscious life, for fear of foreclosing the patient's wish to reveal his inner world. At the same time, the therapist, who cannot conceive of conscious life without unconscious life, hopes to re-connect to this claim upon which psychoanalytic theory rests. Thus begins the quest to discover and reveal disparate and split-off parts of human experience, reaffirming the value of the meaning of mental life like the air we breathe.

The first impressions that the patient makes are like finger-prints. Each beginning is unique, and at first the therapist resists conscious thoughts of reconciliation with hundreds of other familiar beginnings. This "wait and see" is unnerving for some patients, as they experience some pressure to reveal themselves. At first the patient may be frightened but will make a start when he realizes that the therapist has found a way of unintrusively signalling that she is also aware of this unsociable beginning. At all times the therapist is carefully observant, taking in how the patient begins. Both parties already begin to be affected by the experience. Strange things happen: the patient may start to inter-view the therapist, refuse to speak, complain about the setting, or do anything but say why he has come. He still looks for some reassurance from the therapist, who continues to help him in his loneliness and fear, without stifling portentous moments. How much is said, how much is conveyed by gesture, and how much is felt creates the fingerprint-like quality of this meeting.

Beginnings are manifold in their complexity and variation. Often a person coming to an assessment has never spoken to a psychotherapist before and does not know what to expect. The couch in the room may come as a surprise, is often ignored, or may be a source of embarrassment. Arriving late or early, not knowing what to say, wanting an immediate solution, questioning the therapist about his qualifications or technique, all present as com-mon challenges to the boundaries of the assessment consultation. A patient may be in an acute anxiety state and magically expect the assessor to change that by telling him what to do. This kind of request is sometimes linked to questions as to whether the psycho-therapist hypnotizes people or demands for a wholly practical approach. Anxious patients sometimes hire a taxi to bring them and take them away; taxi drivers rarely understand the nature of an assessment for psychotherapy and may return early to collect their fare.

Sometimes, a patient may become upset in a first session, having got in touch with feelings that have been buried for a long time. In the assessment the patient tries to assemble himself under the pressure of his history, losses, failures, and fears for the future.

Somewhere in the assessment, all these may converge in hope and despair. Often the possibility of therapy is a last resort, and in an assessment a patient may admit to having suicidal feelings never before disclosed. He brings to this session his bewilderment about multiple relationships, clandestine and divided worlds of home, work, and a secret life, but he is terrified at knowing what it means.

Then there are the patients who have been in therapy before and have gained a certain expertise. This emanates from the patient's presentation of himself, sometimes with an apology and shame but at others with an absence of any mystery or respect for the unknown. There are those who are so ill that referral to a psychiatrist is needed, and this has to be worked at and faced within the session. All the difficulties may also be opportunities to help the patient through the assessment and enable him to leave the session with self-respect and to take away something that is helpful. In the private setting, the assessor and the patient are alone with each other, with each being deeply aware of the other.

Unlike the intense and in-depth work that Murray Jackson and his team carried out (Jackson & Williams, 1994), the BAP Clinical Service provides assessment, not diagnosis. In my view, a clinical service should share the commitment to offer a dynamic understanding to a patient, no matter what the aetiology of the presenting problems. This is part of my interpretation of a principal aim, "to promote the practice of psychotherapy so as to bring it within reach of a wider section of the community". This aim seems to be the more ambitious today because it was formulated in a climate of relative stability, not only in the domain of psychoanalysis but with regard to the availability of psychological treatments. The difference today is that there has been a reduction of a system of national care and a change in the economic culture on the one hand and, on the other, an increase in psychological treatments available. Thus the aim of *promoting psychotherapy* is even more important, given that psychoanalytic therapy risks becoming diminished by a collection of derivatives and other unrecognizable treatments.

There are two issues to be stressed. The first is the one to which this whole book is devoted—the detailed elaboration of the special meeting that occurs between the assessor of the Clinical

Service and the prospective patient, as discussed in detail from a technical, procedural, and therapeutic point of view throughout this book. The meeting is particularly special because it may become the one that is instrumental in making a difference to a person's life. The belief that this can be achieved through such a meeting is subject to the paradoxical position that the patient may well be striving to hold on to that which is most familiar in his experience, in spite of the fact that he comes for help. The consultant psychotherapist recognizes this and may surprise the patient when she draws attention to it by acknowledging early on the patient's anxiety in the meeting. As the patient realizes that he is being heard, he may be able to say more about what he hears and feels in himself.

The second issue to stress is that the consultation is a cultural and social experience. The fact that organizations offering psychotherapy have proliferated in recent times has to be acknowledged. The water has never been clear, since psychoanalysis began, with regard to theoretical, technical, or political allegiances and now is very muddy indeed. This may be of little concern to most patients, but the therapist is well aware of being in a scene of hugely differing treatment modalities, ranging from the physical—as in therapeutic massage and interactive therapies—to the most esoteric. This judgemental and competitive climate is contrary to the aspirations of psychoanalytic psychotherapy and is another threat to the enterprise of helping a patient to have a different appreciation of himself and enter into what Freud once called a "psychical analysis" (1893a).

An assessment is a space within which some thinking may take place and some contact may be made between the therapist and the patient. The beginning is akin to the animal kingdom, which is without words, and other signals are more important such as dress, body language, use of the consulting-room, and how physical distances between the two people are maintained. It seems like a dance at first, but this self-consciousness dissipates as more and more thoughts flow and words become possible. Nevertheless, we cannot take for granted the implications of a man and a woman, or a man and a man, or a woman and a woman being alone in a room together. Differences of culture, gender, and language all have to be allowed for in thinking about the meaning of things. Even within our own culture, there is a vast range of expectations, some people being quite comfortable with the psychoanalytic world, the cost of sessions, ideas of free association, and interpretation of dreams, whilst others are unfamiliar with it and may be anxious or hostile.

Important to many patients is whether they will be found acceptable, given that personal unacceptability has brought them to the assessment consultation. Yet there is strange incongruity about this, as very few patients will know of Bion's (1967) idea that, if treatment ever begins, it will be because the therapy itself becomes problematic. In other words, sooner or later the patient will blame the psychotherapist for what has happened in his life: everything that is unacceptable in the patient's life will find its way into the therapy. Nevertheless, consciously the patient seeks an experience that liberates him from past pain and avoids repetitions. The representatives of these strivings are found in patients who search for a specific type of therapist regarding concerns such as gender, age, or orientation, and only at the beginning might it be possible for the patient to indulge in this. This is a conscious attempt to rewrite history, revealing the patient's inner desires which are usually expressed as an unanalysed "shopping list".

An assessment is a space with a background of great complexity and conflicting issues, but, as mentioned before, the first contacts with the patient should be treated by the therapist in the same way that a careful detective regards clear fingerprints. Although each beginning is unique, it is difficult to resist making comparisons, and frequently, at an early stage in the consultation, the patient will be seeking clarifications that are often hidden pressures to avoid dealing with what are the really important issues. The therapist retains a careful observance over both herself and the patient. These are precious moments. When the patient begins to realize that the therapist is in fact so attentive, perhaps noticing that it is in a particular way, listening, absorbing detail, he also realizes that he is being given unusual attention.

When the patient begins to talk and question for himself how he is going to use the session, the sense is of a beginning. The therapist uses her skills of "not knowing, not anticipating, and not judging" what is to come. The patient becomes a contradiction in

his own terms before he knows it. He says, "I had a normal childhood and I do not know why I am here", but he has brought
himself to a psychotherapist. He may say, " I had a terrible childhood and my life is a hopeless mess", but if he believed this abso-
lutely would he come to the psychoanalytic psychotherapist? The
patient who says, "This is the therapy of the last resort" protects
his hopefulness in case the therapist will not sustain him in this
belief because she does not realize that he, the patient, is more
hopeful than the therapist. With contradictions, the patient comes
"to make sense of nonsense" by reconciling his experience of life
outside with what is felt inside. Patients bring the most fundamental of problems, where the weight given to either the outside world
or the inside world is such that it imperils one and exaggerates the
other. The sense of self becomes threatened; the ability to make
sense of the world reduces in proportion to increasing feelings of
failure and alienation. In order to reach the way a patient feels, we
question singular rationalist approaches to life that have already
failed him. We find ourselves thinking about and attempting to
discuss basic needs in life such as eating, feeding, sleeping, relationships, sex, and using power. We may ask what these mean and
what form they take in a person's life. In this way, during the
assessment, ideas are acquired about the nature of the patient's
"intercourse with the world" whilst the patient tells us about his
life.

A person comes for an assessment precisely because he cannot
see his own life clearly.

A woman patient, whom I shall call Miss A, could not understand why she had had so many relationships with men but
had never been able to settle down. She began, for the first
time, to talk with real feeling about her father's death when
she was 7 years old. Her mother, locked into a permanent state
of grief, had never been able to move on from the idealized
memory of Miss A's father. The patient became racked with
guilt whenever she began to enjoy a man's company. This had
become such an entrenched pattern that it appeared to be the
problem in itself, so that Miss A was very reluctant to open
feelings about her relationship with her mother or memories of

her father. In the assessment there was an antagonism towards the therapist, as though he should not have disturbed the status quo. At one point, she said that her intelligence was being insulted and got up to leave. The therapist remained seated and said: "It seems as though something very frightening but also important has happened and you are being driven by your guilty feelings." This was a desperate intervention, at a desperate moment. Whether or not the words meant anything to the patient will never be known, but the therapist's composure and remaining firm was what seemed to matter. The rest of the assessment was taken up with the patient's distress, but there was an increasing sense of her living out a part of her life—that of being anchored to the unexpressed grief of her mother before she could really reach her own. After the assessment, the patient sought a referral to a psychotherapist for long-term therapy.

The end of the assessment session is as important as the beginning, but it is different in a significant way. By the end, the therapist will have substantially increased her knowledge of the patient, disproportionately to the patient's knowledge of the therapist. He will find himself having to trust the therapist, perhaps with some comfort that the therapist is a relative stranger. The patient's knowledge will have increased to the extent that, for example, Miss A began to grasp not only something about the nature of the psychotherapeutic relationship, but also a sense of how her problems could be experienced in a relationship that does not have to end in a rejection. In her case, her expectation was, as always, that her overwhelming feelings could not be understood and therefore could not be responded to. It was very difficult for her to leave the session, but she also knew that she was not being rejected. She had obtained for herself a *sense of meaning* as a result of the assessment, which she could take forward.

Freud's use of the word "psychical" (1893a, 1895c [1894]) in early papers is historic but also reminds us of the roots of psychoanalysis. It prompts a reflection on the nature of the assessment session as a space for thinking and feeling, when so often in a medical setting a concrete and immediate response is demanded.

The confidence to use a thinking and feeling space has to be acquired in psychoanalytic work. In these terms, the assessment is a *"psychical event"*. Much more is happening at that time than either the therapist or the patient can know for themselves. In spite of all these difficulties of *completing a task of assessment*, each patient may be able to take away his own sense of "the event", when the therapist is able to contain and sometimes reveal aspects of the psychical as he works through feelings to find thought and words.

CHAPTER NINE

Contraindications
for psychodynamic psychotherapy

Mira Malovic-Yeeles

> "She must try to get hold of something that evaded her. . . .
> Phrases came. Visions came. Beautiful phrases. But what she
> wished to get hold of was the very jar on the nerves, the thing
> itself, before it has been made anything"
>
> Virginia Woolf, "To the Lighthouse"

C ontraindications? Are there any? Wouldn't everybody
benefit from psychotherapy?
It all depends on the kind of psychotherapy. Here, we
are talking about individual psychoanalytic and analytic psychotherapy in an out-patient private practice setting. It is suitable for
many patients, but "the risk of poor judgement is not merely
therapeutic failure, but disaster" (Crown, 1983).

Very few psychotherapists agree with Robert Langs, who
wrote in 1982: "A therapist has an ethical responsibility to take
into therapy all patients who enter his or her office". Such a
therapist needs to be able to assess difficult cases and embark on
them with her eyes open and with appropriate modifications in
technique. At present, apart from modern pharmacotherapies,

other methods of psychological treatment which might be "more convenient" could include individual psychotherapy of one or other variety, group therapy, behaviour therapy, and family and marital therapy.

Most psychoanalytic and analytic psychotherapists look for some criteria on which selection for psychoanalytic and analytic therapy may be based. The problem of selecting adult patients for psychoanalytic therapy is beset with confusion. In the psychoanalytic literature, many different criteria have been put forward on which selection may be based, and a variety of different terms have been used to describe the different aspects of the selection process.

Confusion about terminology

There is some confusion in the literature between indications/ contraindications on the one hand, and criteria of suitability/unsuitability on the other. Freud introduced the term *indication* from the classical medical model, meaning that both the patient's history and his symptoms suggest a disorder for which therapy would be appropriate. *Contraindication* suggests that a particular treatment should not be employed. Terminological distinctions between symptoms (something of which the patient complains) and signs (something elicited from the patient by examination) is not always maintained, although this difference is of crucial importance. While criteria of suitability reflect assessment of the patient's qualities and capacities to form a therapeutic alliance, this chapter is chiefly concerned with contraindications for psychodynamic psychotherapy.

Most psychoanalysts regard the presence of psychiatric illness as a contraindication for psychoanalysis on the basis of the patient's symptoms and criteria of suitability, which, in this situation, overlap. The mental state of the psychiatric patient is usually such that he lacks the necessary requirements for sustaining a treatment alliance (Sandler, Holder, & Dare, 1970). The latter is regarded as necessary in order to enable the patient to cooperate in treatment, to deal with transference phenomena as they emerge, and to gain, and retain, insight. However, not all authors agree that an active psychosis is a contraindication for psychoanalysis, or that the presence of a psychotic illness implies that the patient is unsuitable for psychoanalytic therapy (Rosen, 1946; Rosenfeld, 1952, 1965, 1969; Searles, 1961, 1963, 1965; Sullivan, 1931).

It would appear that some of the problems in this area could be clarified if the distinction between *indications* and *criteria of suitability* was maintained. The question would not be whether psychotic patients are treatable by psychoanalysis, but whether any particular psychotic patient shows the presence or absence of those qualities necessary for the formation of a therapeutic alliance. Mental deficiency is generally regarded as a contraindication for psychoanalysis, not because of the symptoms calling for treatment, but because of the patient's low intelligence. The crucial question is whether this is too low for the patient to form an adequate treatment alliance, and, in particular, whether he is thought to have the capacity to develop a sufficient degree of insight.

As early as 1895, Freud expressed his concern about the selection of patients for psychoanalysis; he used the term "suitable" (1895d). In 1904 he wrote about the nature of the analytic method involving indications and contraindications with respect to the person to be treated, as well as with respect to the clinical picture (1904a). In 1905 he remarked, "Psychoanalysis should not be attempted when the speedy removal of dangerous symptoms is required" (1905a). Jung, in "Aims of Psychotherapy" (1931), talks about *"indicia"* for therapy—for example, age, temperament (introverted/extroverted), attitudes (spiritual/materialistic)—but he also explains that, although *"indicium"* might appear to mean, as in medical parlance generally, that this or that treatment is indicated, psychotherapy has reached no such degree of certainty and therefore *"indicia"* are not much more than mere warnings against one-sidedness.

Further terms used by Freud were "accessible" and "inaccessible". The notion of "accessibility" as a quality of the patient is in current use. It is defined as the patient's ability to think in "psychological terms" and see connections between events and feelings in himself. Inability to think in "psychological" terms is referred to as a "lack of psychological grasp" (Joseph, 1967). Fenichel (1945) referred to general accessibility of the patient without specifying the nature of "accessibility". Glover (1954a) took the term "accessible" to apply particularly to the patient's crucial ability to form a workable transference relationship. Accessibility is not an alternative term to *suitability*. In "Indications for Psychoanalysis", Joseph (1967) introduced the term *"analysability"*, reflecting the features considered under "suitability" rather than putting the main focus on the patient's symptoms. Analysability is currently a popular term in discussion of the criteria for selecting patients for psychoanalysis.

*"Sick enough to need it
and healthy enough to stand it"
(Kächele & Thomä, 1987)*

Selection for psychotherapy involves not only assessment of the patient's capacity to tolerate the undertaking, which could be potentially hazardous, it also involves matching him to a therapist who can contain him without being harmed emotionally or physically himself.

As described in chapter one, we can see that the literature is extensive around criteria for selection, based on the patient's characteristics, the therapist's techniques, or the interaction between patient and therapist. From this we form our framework for assessment both for suitability and unsuitability, learning to recognize the contraindications for referral for analytic or psychoanalytic psychotherapy.

Already in 1935, Jung wrote that "psychotherapy is not the single, straightforward method people at first believed it to be, but, as has gradually become clear, a kind of dialectical process, a dialogue or discussion between two persons" (p. 3). In the doctor-patient relationship, two psychic systems interact; therefore, any deeper insight into the psychotherapeutic process will infallibly reach the conclusion that, in the last analysis, since individuality is a fact not to be ignored, the relationship must be dialectical. Freud (1937c) wrote in "Analysis Terminable and Interminable" about the influence of the personality of the analyst on the efficacy of an analysis. Fenichel (1945) referred to the fact that a particular analyst may have limitations with regard to a patient with certain kinds of problems, whilst the same patient may be successfully analysed by another analyst. Someone who can work with violent patients may well not tolerate a silent patient. Working with severely and profoundly handicapped children and adults who are also emotionally disturbed is a very specific application of psychoanalytical psychotherapy (Sinason, 1992). Pollock (1960) drew attention to the fact that the patient's "specification" for a therapist may have some validity. The view that such initial reaction is evidence of resistance and defensiveness leads to a disregard of this possibility. A patient may be wrongly labelled as unsuitable because of his failure to develop a treatment alliance with that analyst, and analysis may fail. Greenson (1967) recognized that the "real" relationship between analyst and patient may contain elements that will make analysis unlikely to be successful.

While it is difficult to have absolute guidelines for contraindications, nevertheless it is possible to indicate certain areas of psychopathology and personal circumstances that give rise to serious doubts as to suitability. Comparatively clear-cut would be a patient with organic brain damage, which would almost certainly preclude this form of psychotherapy. In the same way, "feeblemindedness" may be said to operate against the choice of analysis as a suitable treatment method. However, Carvalho (1985) wrote that the patient does not require a high I.Q. for psychotherapy, but simply the capacity to "see" what the therapist may be getting at and the ability to relate to it.

Psychosis will generally be regarded as a contraindication, although there are notable exceptions to this. The ability to distinguish between internal and external reality is a major criterion for analysability. It is the essence of the capacity to distinguish between transference neurosis and the therapeutic alliance. It is also worth bearing in mind that patients with an unstable psychosis might get worse.

Brooke (1994) described structural differences in pathologies "of the self" and "within the self". Patients with self-cohesion feel as if they have a self that is embodied, spacious, and bounded. For a relatively cohesive patient, problems lie "within" the self, and they experience conflict. For such a patient, interpretations of defence are likely momentarily to increase the experience of conflict, then lead to a sense of relief. Patients who suffer with a fundamental pathology of the self feel split, fragmented, or precariously unstable most of the time, persecuted from within and without. The body feels alien or robot-like, and the person may feel depersonalized or unreal, ungrounded, with poor boundaries. There is a longing to be understood, yet a terror of being swallowed by others' understanding. There is a desire to feel autonomous and independent, yet a terror of being abandoned. Separation and loss are an unbearable pain. For such a patient, an interpretation of defence is more likely to lead to regression, which may include increasing fragmentation and a deterioration in functioning.

Some patients, however, who have had schizophrenic symptoms might still be suitable for intensive psychotherapy, but the psychotic transference may need a more supportive environment than private practice can provide. For example, Jackson (1993) gave an account of a patient suffering from a severe manic-depressive disorder with schizoid features and a family history of manic-depressive illness, who was successfully treated with individual, intensive psychoanalytic psychotherapy in the context of a psychodynamic psychiatric ward, with encouraging results.

Patients whom we might term borderline may not initially be ready for intensive psychoanalytic work. Josephine Klein (1990), in the paper "Patients Who Are Not Ready for Interpretations", writes about patients for whom interpretations of unconscious material are inappropriate. The common element for these patients is that conditions are not propitious for establishing a therapeutic alliance. They have no understanding of how the therapist and patient interact; no understanding about free association and interpretation; no trust in the object world, where they feel persecuted; and an ego weakness, two aspects of which are a lack of ego-functioning (thinking) and a lack of ego-integration (identity). The therapist has to deal with numerous terrors, feelings of resentment, immense pain, rejection and abandonment, vulnerability, no core, and no sense of identity.

To have a seriously damaged patient in private practice who has no close attachments and little or no social network can put a heavy burden on the therapist and will affect the capacity for change. Carvalho (1985) describes psychotherapy as an empathic relationship whereby it becomes possible to relate to the disavowed aspects of the self. Encountering feared mental contents carries a potentially high risk of side effects. The patient can become psychotic or totally dependent upon the therapist, suicidal, or violent to others, including the therapist, and the disturbance may become worse. The chaotic, deprived personality may experience even an ordinary doctor–patient relationship as provocative. The idealized person of the therapist evokes unfulfillable longings of childhood combined with an overwhelming degree of affects in anticipation of certain disappointment. To put it another way, McDougall (1989) asks whether the psychoanalytic situation is bearable. Can the patient accept a situation in which he is asked to say everything that comes to mind, but not act on it? Can he tolerate the therapist not gratifying his wishes and needs directly? If the patient is able to withstand these painful aspects of the analytic relationship, are we willing to engage with him even if he is difficult?

Today, a patient's total lack of willingness to take responsibility for his own personal evolution might be said to present a serious contraindication. Previously, Freud (1904a) wrote that if the physician has to deal with a worthless character, he soon loses the interest that makes it possible to enter profoundly into the patient's mental life. Jones (1920) agreed, but pointed out that much better results can be achieved with "worthwhile characters". Fenichel (1945) referred to the fact that a particular analyst may have limitations with regard to a patient who displays certain problems. This view suggests that a patient who is regarded as having a certain type of "moral deficiency" may be unacceptable to one analyst whilst being capable of being successfully analysed by another. Saul (1958) felt the analyst to be irresponsible if he did not choose his patients with some idea of their potential contribution to society in mind. However, Sterba (1969) thought that the analyst must learn to set aside the moral appraisal of patients.

The hardest part of an assessment is to have to say "No". Patients have waited to be seen and have invested high hopes in their assessment. However, when one is reasonably certain that this kind of therapy is not suitable, and may even be damaging, then "No" is the only response. One needs to know about other possible therapies and approaches that could be helpful, and refer the patient in another direction, but if there is no known therapy suitable for the patient, it is necessary to say so. It helps to underline that therapy is not suitable for him, rather than that he is not suitable for therapy. The most difficult and uncomfortable feeling is recognition and acknowledgement that we, as psychotherapists, are not omnipotent.

The contraindications for and possible dangers of psychotherapy

The contraindications for and dangers of psychotherapy are important to consider, and the literature on them is predominantly American in origin, with a few recent publications from the United Kingdom. Psychotherapy, like any other effective treatment in medicine, may lead to negative effects either in the patient or in those around him. Some transitory negative effects may be not only an accepted, but also an expected outcome of the psychotherapeutic process. The viewpoints on what comprises a negative effect of psychotherapy may, and frequently do, differ. Changes in an insecure, anxious, drawn, depressed housewife to a more assertive, self-assured wife, insisting on a more egalitarian relationship with her husband, will challenge his power and dominance. The husband might regard this as a negative effect, whereas she might consider it as the most important thing she has ever done.

Therefore, the repercussions of psychotherapy need to be subdivided into personal repercussions and the effects on others. Personal repercussions may include the appearance of new and more severe neurotic symptoms, or even a psychosis. Psychotherapy for psychosomatic conditions can put life at risk from well-recognized medical and surgical complications of these disorders (asthma attacks, bleeding, ulcerative colitis). Patients with impulsive or histrionic personalities can indulge in dangerous "acting out", such as substance abuse or antisocial, criminal behaviour. Social and family repercussions include changes in the family system through the change in one of its members. A spouse is deserted, and this has an effect on the children. Is a better quality of life for one spouse, or possibly both, worth the break-up of the marriage? Is it better for the children to have two satisfied and fulfilled parents who live separately, or to live in a family unit where the parents are arguing and one parent is always miserable and nobody is happy? All these are ethical dilemmas that we and our patients have to face in order to make a decision for change. Successful therapy brings about changes, not all of which are pleasant or easy.

The source of negative effects may be in the patient, the therapist, the patient–therapist interaction, or the patient's social situation, although the personality of the patient is the most important factor. The influence of the therapist results from his personality, as well as his training and technique. Rigidity of technique is likely to lead to problems. Faulty technique may be said to include excessive intrusiveness; denigrating the patient and damaging his self-esteem; invalidating the patient's experience; the therapist being a "blank screen" rather than a person as well; confusing the patient with conflicting messages or conflicting demands; and having an all-knowing, authoritarian, rigid attitude to theory and technique. The other problem arises from the wrong use of the transference relationship, talking about it as a fact instead of interpreting it in an "as if" manner. Similarly, acting out in the countertransference is possible. Buckley, Karasu, and Charles (1981) found that unresolved transference issues underlie many negative effects.

An absolute contraindication is organic brain disease where, apart from a difficulty in forming a therapeutic alliance, any challenging comment carries the risk of a catastrophic reaction (Lishman, 1980). Relative contraindications for psychotherapy include addiction, serious destructive or self-destructive behaviour suggesting poor frustration tolerance, a history of prolonged psychotic breakdown in the face of stress, and entrenched somatization, with the concomitant "secondary gain".

It is important to take into account the context in which worrying episodes may have taken place. An escalating pattern of active substance abuse, impulsiveness, or illness in response to stress requires utmost caution. Isolated incidents can be taken on their merits. Inclusion and exclusion factors listed in the literature guide the assessor in finding the fulcrum between illness and need on the one hand, and healthy robustness on the other.

> "Of two things we cannot sufficiently beware—of obstinacy if we confine ourselves to our proper field—of inadequacy if we desert it"
>
> Johann Wolfgang von Goethe

Conclusions

Judy Cooper and Helen Alfillé

> "... this strange disease of modern life,
> With its sick hurry, its divided aims ..."
>
> Matthew Arnold, "The Scholar Gypsy"

Perhaps the main conclusion to be drawn from this book is the importance of a thorough assessment before a patient is referred for psychoanalytic psychotherapy. Since Freud, the type of presenting problem has changed dramatically, and the basis on which people are referred for psychoanalytic psycho-therapy has broadened considerably. The scope has increased to include not only the "good neurotic", but also narcissistic and borderline patients with severe problems in functioning. There is also a group of patients who seek therapy not because of incapacitating symptoms, but because they wish to explore conflictual issues in a search for personal growth, which may also help their professional development.

The way in which a problem is formulated in an assessment consultation can have a profound effect on the patient and can be therapeutic in its own right. For instance, a middle-aged woman still living at home with her mother came to an assessment with quite florid presenting symptoms, hearing voices, and with paranoid fantasies. This could have been seen either as an indication of psychotic pathology or as a signal of distress representing a hope that something could be done about the intolerable, trapped situation between daughter and mother. Our decision as assessors will be based on how we read these symptoms—whether we look at them in terms of psychosis or from a more Winnicottian view of a reaching out for help—and consequently will influence any subsequent referral.

The assessment consultation can be seen as a blueprint for any future psychotherapy. From the assessment session, we must make up our minds whether to offer a referral; the difference between assessing for therapy in an institution or clinic, as opposed to that in private practice, must also be borne in mind. We must be cognisant of any contraindications while looking at the potential suitability of a patient. We look for the patient's ability to use an interpretation, to talk of fantasies and dreams, to be aware of unconscious motivation. We must try to assess ego strength (psychoanalytic psychotherapy can be difficult, frustrating, and sometimes painful), and look at the defences that the patient uses. It has to be remembered that defences must be respected—they may be preventing complete disintegration, being used to protect an extremely fragile ego. We need to gauge the patient's ability to tolerate feelings of guilt (has he reached the depressive position?). Can he alternate freely between inner and outer reality, and does he recognize the difference between them? Can he move back and forth in historical time and make connections while relating his history? Above all, is he curious to explore the reasons why he is where he is in his life?

In assessing, just as in long-term psychotherapy, it is important to remember our analytic position at all times:

> What is distinctive about psychotherapy is the therapist's prohibition upon himself from enacting either the promptings of his own inner world or those of his patient. . . . This analysing stance, which runs painfully counter to the way both therapist and patient usually structure their relationships, is

the setting for psychotherapy that I think is most fundamental. [Temperley, 1984, p. 102]

As our clinical experience demonstrates, it is essential to know *how* to conduct an assessment. Our main objective will be to explore the phantasies and object relations of the patient's inner world. However, it is also necessary to get as clear an idea as possible of the setting of his external life: his work, his routines, and, above all, his relationships and more general social network. One learns that to have some creative structures in place augurs well for any future psychotherapy.

The chapters in this book reveal the complexities of this very difficult subject. They explore in depth the assessor's role in the initial consultation. We endeavour to bridge the gap between what a patient may expect (immediate relief of symptoms and a cure) and what we as psychotherapists can offer in terms of a psychodynamic formulation of the patient's situation. This is sometimes therapeutic in its own right, giving the patient a different perspective which may be useful and sufficient, at least for the time being. Those who, we feel, can be referred may decide to take up the offer.

The assessment process starts with the patient's fantasy about psychotherapy, before any contact is made with an assessor. With the *name* of the assessor—and, therefore, an object to attach to—the emerging transference deepens. From the assessor's point of view, the conversation with or the message left by the patient will be a relevant part of the assessment. Perhaps it is worth remembering that this first unseen, aural contact between patient and assessor is a repetition evocative of one of the earliest prenatal links between infant and mother.

REFERENCES

Aarons, Z. A. (1962). Indications for analysis and problems of analyzability. *Psychoanalytic Quarterly, 31*: 514–531.

Abraham, K. (1919). The applicability of psychoanalytic therapy to patients of advanced age. In: *Selected Papers on Psycho-Analysis.* London: Hogarth Press [reprinted London: Karnac Books, 1979].

Bachrach, H., & Leaff, L. (1978). Analysability: a systematic review of the clinical and quantitative literature. *Journal of the American Psychoanalytic Association, 26*: 881–920.

Bachrach, H. M., Weber, J., & Solomon, M. (1985). Factors associated with the outcome of psychoanalysis (clinical and methodological considerations): Report of the Columbia Psychoanalytic Center Research Project IV. *International Review of Psycho-Analysis, 12*: 379–389.

Baker, R. (1980). The finding of "not suitable" in the selection of supervised cases. *International Review of Psycho-Analysis, 7*: 353–364.

Balint, M. (1950). Changing therapeutic aims and techniques in psychoanalysis. *International Journal of Psycho-Analysis, 31*: 117–124.

Bandler, R., & Grindler, J. (1975). *The Patterns of the Hypnotic Techniques of Milton H. Erikson, M.D., Vol. 1.* Palo Alto, CA: Behaviour and Science Books.

139

Bateman, A., & Holmes, J. (1995). *Introduction to Psychoanalysis*. London: Routledge.

Bibring, E. (1937). Symposium on the theory of the therapeutic results of psycho-analysis. *International Journal of Psycho-Analysis, 18*: 170–189.

Bion, W. (1962). *Learning from Experience*. London: Heinemann [reprinted London: Karnac Books, 1984].

Bion, W. (1967). *Second Thoughts*. London: Heinemann [reprinted London: Karnac Books, 1984].

Bleger, J. (1967). Psychoanalysis of the psychoanalytic frame. *International Journal of Psycho-Analysis, 48*: 511–519.

Bloch, S. (1979). Assessment of patients for psychotherapy. *British Journal of Psychiatry, 135*: 193–208.

Brooke, R. (1994). Assessment for psychotherapy: clinical indicators of self-cohesion and self-pathology. *British Journal of Psychotherapy, 10* (3): 317–329.

Brown, D., & Pedder, J. (1979). *Introduction to Psychotherapy*. London: Tavistock.

Buckley, P., Karasu, T. B., & Charles, E. (1981). Psychotherapists view their personal therapy. *Psychotherapy: Theory, Research & Practice, 18*: 299–305.

Carvalho, R. (1985). The selection of patients for psychotherapy. *Practical Reviews in Psychiatry*, No. 10.

Coltart, N. (1983). Diagnosis and assessment of suitability for psychoanalytic psychotherapy. *British Association of Psychotherapists Bulletin, 14*, 1–9.

Coltart, N. (1987). Diagnosis and assessment of suitability for psychoanalytic psychotherapy. In: *Slouching Towards Bethlehem and Further Psychoanalytic Explorations*. London: Free Association Books, 1992.

Coltart, N. (1988). The assessment of psychological-mindedness in the diagnostic interview. *British Journal of Psychiatry, 153*: 819–820.

Coltart, N. (1992). *Slouching Towards Bethlehem and Further Psychoanalytic Explorations*. London: Free Association Books.

Coltart, N. (1993). *How to Survive as a Psychotherapist*. London: Sheldon Press.

Crown, S. (1983). Contra-indications and dangers of psychotherapy. *British Journal of Psychotherapy, 143*: 436–441.

Epstein, R. A. (1990). Assessment and suitability for low-fee control psychoanalysis. *Journal of the American Psychoanalytic Association, 38*: 951–984.

Erle, J., & Goldberg, D. (1979). An approach to the study of analysability and analysis: the course of 40 consecutive cases selected for supervised analysis. *Psychoanalytic Quarterly, 47*: 198–228.

Erle, J., & Goldberg, D. (1984). Assessment of analyzability. *Journal of the American Psychoanalytic Association, 32*: 715–737.

Fenichel, O. (1945). *The Psychoanalytic Theory of Neurosis*. New York: W. W. Norton.

Fordham, M. (1978). *Jungian Psychotherapy*. London: Wiley [reprinted London: Karnac Books, 1986].

Frank, J. (1956). Indications and contraindications for the standard technique. *Journal of the American Psychoanalytic Association, 4*: 266–284.

Freud, A. (1954). The widening scope of indications for psychoanalysis. *Journal of the American Psychoanalytic Association, 2*: 607–620. Also in: *The Widening Scope of Indications for Analysis: Indications for Child Analysis*. London. Hogarth Press, 1969.

Freud, S. (1893a) (with Breuer, J.). On the psychical mechanism of hysterical phenomena: preliminary communication. In: *The Standard Edition of the Complete Psychological Works of Sigmund Freud*, ed. James Strachey. London: Hogarth Press, 1953–73, Vol. 2.

Freud, S. (1895a). The psychotherapy of hysteria. *S.E., 2*.

Freud, S. (1895c [1894]). Obsessions and phobias: their psychical mechanism and their aetiology. *S.E., 3*.

Freud, S. (1895d) (with Breuer, J.). *Studies on Hysteria. S.E., 2*.

Freud, S. (1896c). The aetiology of hysteria. *S.E., 3*.

Freud, S. (1904a). Freud's psycho-analytic procedure. *Standard Edition 7*.

Freud, S. (1905a). On psychotherapy *S.E., 7*.

Freud, S. (1905e [1901]). Fragment of an analysis of a case of hysteria. *S.E., 7*.

Freud, S. (1912e). Recommendations to physicians practising psychoanalysis. *S.E., 12*.

Freud, S. (1913c). On beginning the treatment. *S.E., 12*.

Freud, S. (1919h). The uncanny. *S.E., 17*.

Freud, S. (1923c [1922]). Remarks on theory and practice of dream-interpretation. *S.E., 19*.

Freud, S. (1926d [1925]). *Inhibitions, Symptoms and Anxiety. S.E., 20*.

Freud, S. (1926e). *The Question of Lay Analysis. S.E., 20*.

Freud, S. (1937c). Analysis terminable and interminable *S.E., 23*.

Garelick, A. (1994). Psychotherapy assessment: theory and practice. *Psychoanalytic Psychotherapy, 8* (2): 101–116.

Glover, E. (1954a). *Technique of Psychoanalysis*. New York: International Universities Press.

Glover, E. (1954b). The indications for psychoanalysis. *Journal of Mental Science, 100*: 393–401.

Gordon, P. (1993). Souls in armour: thoughts on psychoanalysis and racism. *British Journal of Psychotherapy, 10* (1): 62–75.

Green, A. (1986). *On Private Madness*. London: Hogarth Press [reprinted London: Karnac Books, 1997].

Greenacre, P. (1966). Problems of overidealization of the analyst and of analysis. *Psychoanalytic Study of the Child, 12*.

Greenson, R. R. (1967). *The Technique and Practice of Psycho-Analysis, Vol. 1*. London: Hogarth Press.

Greenson, R. R. (1992). *The Technique and Practice of Psychoanalysis, Vol. 2: A Memorial Volume to Ralph R. Greenson*, ed. Alan Sugarman, Robert A. Nemiroff, & Daniel P. Greenson. Madison, CT: International Universities Press.

Guex, P. (1989). *An Introduction to Psycho-Oncology*, transl. by Heather Goodare. London: Routledge, 1994.

Hinshelwood, R. D. (1995). Psychodynamic formulation in assessment for psychoanalytic psychotherapy. In: C. Mace (Ed.), *The Art and Science of Assessment in Psychotherapy*. London: Routledge.

Holmes, J. (1995). How I assess for psychoanalytic psychotherapy. In: C. Mace (Ed.), *The Art and Science of Assessment in Psychotherapy*. London: Routledge.

Huxster, H., Lower, R., & Escott, P. (1975). Some pitfalls in assessment of analyzability in a psychoanalytic clinic. *Journal of the American Psychoanalytic Association, 23*: 90–106.

Jackson, M. (1993). Manic-depressive psychosis, psychopathology and individual psychotherapy within a psychodynamic milieu. *Psychoanalytical Psychotherapy, 7* (2): 103–133.

Jackson, M., & Williams, P. (1994). *Unimaginable Storms*. London: Karnac Books.

Jones, E. (1920). *Treatment of Neuroses*. London: Bailliere, Tindall & Cox.

Joseph, B. (1983). On understanding and not understanding. some technical issues. *International Journal of Psycho-Analysis, 64*.

Joseph, B. (1985). Transference: the total situation. *International Journal of Psycho-Analysis, 66*: 447–454.

Joseph, E. D. (Ed.) (1967). *Indications for Psychoanalysis*. Monograph 2, Kris Study Group of the New York Psychoanalytic Institute. New York: International Universities Press.

Jung, C. G. (1928). Psychoanalysis and the cure of souls. *C.W., Vol. 11.*

Jung, C. G. (1931). Aims of psychotherapy. *C.W., Vol. 16.*

Jung, C. G. (1933). *Modern Man in Search of a Soul.* London: Routledge & Kegan Paul, 1961.

Jung, C. G. (1935). Principles of practical psychotherapy. *C.W., Vol. 16.*

Jung, C. G. (1945/1948). On the nature of dreams. *C.W., Vol. 8.*

Kächele, H., & Thomä, H. (1987). *Psychoanalytic Practice.* New York: Springer Verlag.

Kantrowitz, J. (1987). Suitability for psychoanalysis. In: R. Langs (Ed.), *The Yearbook of Psychoanalysis and Psychotherapy* (pp. 403–416). London/New York: Gardner.

Kantrowitz, J., Katz, A. L., Greenhan, D., Morris, H., Paolitto, F., Sashin, O., & Solomon, L. (1989). The patient–analyst match and the outcome of psychoanalysis: a pilot study. *Journal of the American Psychoanalytic Association, 37:* 893–920.

Kernberg, O., Burnstein, E., Coyne, L., Appelbaum, A., Horowitz, L., Voth, H. (1972). Psychotherapy and psychoanalysis. Final part of the Menninger Foundation's psychotherapy research project. *Bulletin of the Menninger Clinic, 36:* 1–275.

Klauber, J. (1971). Personal attitudes to psychoanalytic consultation. In: *Difficulties in the Analytic Encounter* (pp. 141–159). New York: Jason Aronson, 1981.

Klauber, J. (1972). On the relationship of transference and interpretation in psychoanalytic therapy. *International Journal of Psycho-Analysis, 53:* 385–392.

Klauber, J. (1981). *Difficulties in the Analytic Encounter.* New York: Jason Aronson [reprinted London: Karnac Books, 1986].

Klein, J. (1990). Patients who are not ready for interpretations. *British Journal of Psychotherapy, 7* (1): 38–49.

Knapp, P. H., Levin, S., McCarter, R. H., Wetment, H., & Zetzel, E. (1960). Suitability for psychoanalysis: a review of one hundred supervised analytic cases. *Psychoanalytic Quarterly, 29:* 459–477.

Kristeva, J. (1983). *Histoires d'amour.* Paris: Editions Denoel.

Kubie, L. (1948). Symposium on the evaluation of therapeutic results. *International Journal of Psycho-Analysis, 29:* 7–33.

Langs, R. (1978). *The Listening Process.* New York: Jason Aronson.

Langs, R. (1982). *Psychotherapy: A Basic Trust.* New York: Jason Aronson.

Langs, R., & Stone, L. (1980). *The Therapeutic Experience and its Setting.* New York: Jason Aronson.

Laufer, M. E., & Laufer, M. (1996). The aim of psychoanalysis. *The Institute of Psycho-Analysis News*, London.

Liberman, D. (1968). Comment on Dr Waldhorn's paper. *International Journal of Psycho-Analysis, 48*: 362–363.

Limentani, A. (1972). The assessment of analysability: a major hazard in selection for psychoanalysis. In: *Between Freud and Klein*. London: Free Association Books, 1989.

Limentani, A. (1989). *Between Freud and Klein*. London: Free Association Books.

Lishman, A. L. (1980). *Organic Psychiatry*. Oxford: Blackwell Scientific Publications.

Little, M. (1951). Countertransference and the patient's response to it. *International Journal of Psycho-Analysis, 32*: 32–40. Also in: R. Langs (Ed.), *Classics in Psychoanalytic Technique*. New York: Jason Aronson, 1981.

Lorenz, K. (1963). *On Aggression*. London: UP, Methuen & Co, 1966.

Mace, C. (Ed.) (1995). *The Art and Science of Assessment in Psychotherapy*. London: Routledge.

Malan, D. H. (1967). *Individual Psychotherapy and the Science of Psychodynamics*. London: Butterworth.

McDougall, J. (1989). *Theatres of the Body*. London: Free Association Books.

Modell, A. (1988). The centrality of the psychoanalytic setting. *Psycho-Analytic Quarterly, 58*: 577–596.

Namnum, R. (1968). The problem of analysability and the autonomous ego. *International Journal of Psycho-Analysis, 49*: 271–275.

Neumann, E. (1954). *The Origins and History of Consciousness*. London: Routledge & Kegan Paul.

Ogden, T. (1989). *The Primitive Edge of Experience*. London: Karnac Books.

Panel (1981). Insight: clinical conceptualizations. *Journal of the American Psychoanalytic Association, 26*: 659–671.

Phillips, A. (1996). You should see in his bedroom . . . Why we need clutter. *The Observer Review* (27 October), pp. 5–6.

Pollock, G. H. (1960). The role and responsibilities of the psychoanalytic consultant. *International Journal of Psycho-Analysis, 41*: 633–636.

Quinodoz, D. (1992). Psychoanalytic setting as instrument of the container function. *International Journal of Psycho-Analysis, 73*: 627–636.

Reich, W. (1933). *Character Analysis*. London: Vision, 1950.

Rickman, J. (1951). Number and the human sciences. In: *Psychoanalysis and Culture*. New York: International Universities Press.

Rosen, J. (1946). A method of resolving acute catatonic excitement. *Psychoanalytic Quarterly, 20*: 183–198.

Rosenfeld, H. A. (1952). Transference phenomena and transference-analysis in an acute catatonic patient. *International Journal of Psycho-Analysis, 33*: 457–464.

Rosenfeld, H. A. (1965). *Psychotic States: A Psychoanalytic Approach*. London: Hogarth Press [reprinted London: Karnac Books, 1982].

Rosenfeld, H. A. (1969). The treatment of psychotic states by psychoanalysis: an historical approach. *International Journal of Psycho-Analysis, 50*: 615–631.

Sanders, K., (1986). *A Matter of Interest: Clinical Notes of a Psychoanalyst in General Practice*. Strathclyde: Clunie Press.

Sandler, J., Dare, C., & Holder, A. (1973). *The Patient and the Analyst*. London: Karnac Books [revised edition, 1992].

Sandler, J., Holder, A., &. Dare, C. (1970). Basic psychoanalytic concepts: the treatment alliance. *British Journal of Psychiatry, 116*: 555–558.

Sashin, J. I., Eldred, S. H., & Van Amerongen, S. T. (1975). A search for predictive factors in institute supervised cases: a retrospective study of 183 cases from 1959–1966 at the Boston Psychoanalytic Society & Institute. *International Journal of Psycho-Analysis, 56*: 343–359.

Saul, L. J. (1958). *Technique and Practice of Psychoanalysis*. Philadelphia, PA: Lippincott.

Schubart, W. (1989). The patient in the psychoanalyst's consulting room: the first consultation as a psychoanalytic encounter. *International Journal of Psycho-Analysis, 70*: 423–432.

Searles, H. F. (1961). Phases of patient therapist interaction in the psychotherapy of chronic schizophrenia. *British Journal of Medical Psychology, 34*: 169–193. Also in: *Collected Papers on Schizophrenia and Related Subjects*. New York: International Universities Press [reprinted London: Karnac Books, 1986].

Searles, H. F. (1963). Transference psychosis in the psychotherapy of chronic schizophrenia. *International Journal of Psycho-Analysis, 44*: 249–281. Also in: *Collected Papers on Schizophrenia and Related Subjects*. New York: International Universities Press [reprinted London: Karnac Books, 1986].

Searles, H. F. (1965). *Collected Papers on Schizophrenia and Related Subjects*. New York: International Universities Press [reprinted London: Karnac Books, 1986].

Searles, H. F. (1973). Concerning therapeutic symbiosis. *Annual of Psychoanalysis, 1*: 247–262. Also in: R. Langs (Ed.), *Classics in Psychoanalytic Technique*. New York: Jason Aronson, 1981.

Shapiro, S. (1984). The initial assessment of the patient: a psychoanalytic approach. *International Review of Psycho-Analysis, 11*: 11–25.

Sinason, V. (1992). *Mental Handicap and the Human Condition*. London: Free Association Books.

Steiner, J. (1993). *Psychic Retreats*. London: Routledge.

Sterba, R. (1969). The psychoanalyst in a world of change. *Psychoanalytic Quarterly, 38*: 432–454.

Stone, L. (1954). The widening scope of indications for psychoanalysis. *Journal of the American Psychoanalytic Association, 2*: 567–594.

Sullivan, H. S. (1931). The modified psychoanalytic treatment of schizophrenia. *American Journal of Psychiatry, 11*: 519–540.

Temperley, J. (1984). Settings for psychotherapy. *British Journal of Psychotherapy, 1* (2): 101–111.

Thompson, C. (1938). Notes on the psychoanalytic significance of the choice of analyst. *Psychoanalytic Quarterly, 29*: 478–506.

Tyson, R. L. & Sandler, J. (1971). Problems in the selection of patients for psychoanalysis: comments on the application of the concepts of "indications", "suitability" and "analysability". *British Journal of Medical Psychology, 44*: 211–228.

Waldhorn, H. F. (1960). Assessment of analysability: technical and theoretical observations. *Psychoanalytic Quarterly, 29*: 478–506.

Waldhorn, H. F. (1968). Indications and contraindications: lessons from the second analysis. *International Journal of Psycho-Analysis, 49*: 358–362.

Weber, J. J., Solomon, M., & Bachrach, H. M. (1985). Factors associated with the outcome of psychoanalysis. *International Review of Psycho-Analysis, 12*: 127–141, 251–262.

Wilson, J. (1996). Notes, stories and all that jazz. *Context, 28:* 37–41.

Winnicott, D.W. (1954). Metapsychological and clinical aspects of regression within the psycho-analytical set-up. In: *Through Paediatrics to Psycho-Analysis*. London: Hogarth Press, 1975 [reprinted London: Karnac Books, 1992].

Winnicott, D. W. (1955). Clinical varieties of transference. In: *Through Paediatrics to Psycho-Analysis*. London: Hogarth Press, 1975 [reprinted London: Karnac Books, 1992].

Winnicott, D. W. (1968). Communication between infant and mother, and mother and infant, compared and contrasted. In: *Babies and their Mothers*. London: Free Association Books, 1987.

Zetzel, E. (1965). The theory of therapy in relation to a developmental model of the psychic apparatus. *International Journal of Psycho-Analysis*, 46: 39–52.

Zetzel, E. (1968). The so-called good hysteric. In: *The Capacity for Emotional Growth*. New York: International Universities Press, 1970 [reprinted London: Karnac Books, 1987].

Zetzel, E. (1970). *The Capacity for Emotional Growth*. New York: International Universities Press, 1970 [reprinted London: Karnac Books, 1987].

INDEX

Aarons, Z. A., 19, 20, 27
Abraham, K., 14
accessibility:
  criteria of, 10–23
  definition, 127, 128
  Freud on, 127
  vs. suitability, 128
  See also analysability; suitability
acting out, 55, 132
  in countertransference, 133
  by referrer, 27
adaptive functioning, 16
adaptive regression, 16
addiction(s), 11, 12, 17, 91, 103,
    133
  See also substance abuse
affect organization, 20
age as factor, 10, 14, 21, 30, 127
Alfillé, H., xv, 1–6, 63–68, 135–137
analysability, 13, 14, 19, 128
  prerequisites for, 16, 129
  See also accessibility; suitability

analysis:
  as art, 70
  as dialectical process, 71
  supervised, selection for, 8, 9, 16,
    18, 32
  trial, 29
  See also therapy
analyst:
  –patient match, *see*
      patient–analyst match
  personality of, 9, 23–25, 34, 128,
    133
  role of, 12
  See also therapist
Anna O [Freud's case], 102
anxiety:
  ability to tolerate, 20, 21
  about assessment, 36
  containment of, 43
  hysteria, 10
  separation, 67, 84, 130
Arnold, M., 135

assessment (*passim*):
    consultation, 87–106
        boundaries and difficulties in,
            115–123
        concluding, 102–106, 122–123
        countertransference in,
            107–113
        and diagnosis, 6
        ending of, 85
        environment of, 3
        as "psychical event", 123
        and psychotherapy, 136
        starting, 88–89, 116–118
        transference in, 107–113
    vs. diagnosis, 47–61
    historical origins of, x
    importance of, 135
    methods of, 16
    process, 26–31
        complexity of, 15
        definition, 9
    as therapeutic space, 3
    variations in the purpose of, 16
assessor–analyst relationship, 30
asthma, 44, 132
attachment, of patient, to assessor,
    2, 6, 137
attention, evenly suspended (free
    hovering), of analyst, x, 28
Auden, W. H., 47

Bachrach, H., 16, 21, 22, 26, 29, 33
Baker, R., 10, 18, 32
Balint, M., x, 40
    movement, 45
Bandler, R., 70
Barnard, J., xv, 5, 35–46
basic rule, x
Bateman, A., 64
behaviour therapy, 41
Berkowitz, R., xv, 5, 7–34
Bibring, E., 14
Bion, W., 55, 120
Bleger, J., 91
Bloch, S., 9, 21
body language, importance of, 6

borderline pathology, 2, 5, 15, 17,
    34, 58, 130, 135
brain disease, organic, 129, 133
British Association of
    Psychotherapists (BAP), 36,
        38, 67, 77, 106, 115
    Child and Adolescent Clinic, xiii
    Clinical Service of, xiii, 5, 35, 36,
        37, 89, 118
    orientations of, xiii
    Reduced Fee Scheme, 95
Brooke, R., 129
Brown, D., 99
Bruno, G., 39
Buckley, P., 133

Carroll, L., 35
Carvalho, R., 129, 131
character disorder(s), 10, 11, 17
    narcissistic, 33
Charles, E., 133
"Chicago 7" illnesses, 44
chronic fatigue syndrome, 43
cognitive therapy, 41
Coltart, N., 17, 18, 20, 21, 28, 29, 31,
    34, 55, 61, 72, 78, 88, 93, 105,
    111
communication:
    unconscious, 42
    verbal, 21
compulsion(s), 11, 19
    repetition, 29, 48
confidentiality:
    anxiety about, 50
    issue of, 38
confusional states, 10
containment, therapeutic,
    boundaries and limits of, 4
contraindications:
    for psychoanalysis, 10
    for psychodynamic
        psychotherapy, 125–134
Cooper, J., xv–xvi, 1–6, 63–68,
    135–137
countertransference, xi, 6, 32, 34,
    73, 74, 77, 106

acting out in, 133
in assessment consultation, 18,
    19, 29, 59, 107–113
as diagnostic tool, 101
and referral, 27
role of, xi
and transference, relationship
    between, 3
–transference projections, 72
Crown, S., 125
culture, as factor, 30
cure:
    instant, 39, 63, 67, 107, 137
    in psychotherapy, 12, 29, 53
    talking, 94

dangers of psychotherapy, 132–134
Dare, C., 92, 126
Darwin, C., 39
Davis, A., xvi, 6, 69–85
defence(s):
    assessment of, 4, 16, 18, 19, 78,
        136
    interpretation of, 130
    against loss, 82, 84, 130
    pathological, 82
    primitive, 18, 59
    role of, 39
    against self-knowledge, 54
    splitting as, 66
    structure, psychic, 81
        collapse of, 84
        fragile, 31
        rigid, 100, 111
    working through, 66, 93, 94
delinquency, 17
depression, 10, 17, 103
    endogenous, 11
    neurotic, 11
    tolerance for, 20, 21
depressive position, 4, 136
    as treatment goal, 67
diagnosis, 5, 6, 16, 17, 23
    of false self, 17
    issues of, 13
    limiting nature of, 11, 12, 15

medical, 103
personality behind, 10–15, 32
in psychoanalytic
    psychotherapy, 47–61
differentiation:
    difficulty with, 75, 83
    –individuation, 84
    of self and object, 19
Dora [Freud's case], ix, 102
dream(s):
    analysis of, 91, 99
    importance of, 4, 136
    interpretation of, 120

eating disorders, 43
ego:
    fragile, and defences, 136
    -functioning:
        lack of, 130
        level of, 4
        resilient and flexible, 17
    -integration, lack of, 130
    strength, 16, 18, 21, 22, 32, 49, 78,
        136
Epstein, R. A., 33
Erle, J., 10, 33
Escott, P., 19
ethical considerations, 14
ethology, 39
experience as factor, 30

Farley, L., xiv
feeblemindedness, 129
Fenichel, O., 10, 11, 14, 30, 127, 129,
    131
finances, issue of, 3, 51, 60, 93,
    95–96, 99
fixation hysteria, 10
flight into health, 56
Fordham, M., 82
fragmentation, 130
frame:
    analytic, safety of, 48
    assessment, 6
    unsafe, 70
    See also setting, assessment

Frank, J., 24, 33
free association, 4, 17, 28, 91, 97, 98,
    120, 130
  capacity for, 52
frequency, of treatment sessions,
    63–68, 93–95
Freud, A., 24, 59
Freud, S., 47–49, 59, 104, 126–128,
    135
  on accessibility, 11, 13, 127
  on age limits, 14
  on aims of psychoanalysis, 53, 63
  on analysis:
    as jigsaw puzzle, 101
    as time-consuming, 92, 93
  on analyst's personality, 7, 23, 32,
    128
  cases:
    Anna O, 102
    Dora, ix, 102
  on criteria for suitability, 3, 7, 10,
    14, 127
  on family referral, 27
  on hostile transference, 49
  on hysteria, 102
  on indications, 126
  on motivation, 14
  on motives of human social
    behaviour, 39
  one-person psychology of, x
  on psychical analysis, 119, 122
  on psychoanalysis as time-
    consuming, 63
  on repetition compulsion, 48
  on sympathy for patients, 108
  on treatment of neuroses, 41
  on trial analysis, 29
  on worthless characters, 131
frustration, ability to tolerate, 14,
    20, 21, 133

Garelick, A., 4, 17, 23, 27, 28, 29, 30,
    47
Garfunkel, A., 107
gastric ulcer, 44
Gibran, K., 87

Glover, E., 10, 11, 29, 128
Goethe, J. W. von, 134
Goldberg, D., 10, 33
Gordon, G., Lord Byron, 115
Gordon, P., 83
Green, A., 101
Greenacre, P., 53
Greenson, R. R., 5, 15, 17, 20, 21, 29,
    96, 108, 129
Grindler, J., 70
Guex, P., 44
guilt feelings, ability to tolerate, 136

Hewitt, P., xvi, 6, 115–123
Hinshelwood, R. D., 9, 19, 27, 29, 71
history, patient's:
  genetic, 52
  psychiatric, 52, 91, 103, 130, 133
  relevance of, 19, 20, 52, 68, 117,
    126
  social and developmental, 2
  taking, 2, 16, 19, 28, 29, 51–53, 78,
    90–91, 109
  See also object relation(s), early
Holder, A., 92, 126
holding, 116
  environmental, 67
  as treatment goal, 63
    primary, 67
Holmes, J., 5, 64
honesty, 20
Huxster, H., 19, 20, 21
hypertension, 44
hypochondriasis, 10, 17
hysteria, 10, 11, 102
  anxiety, 10, 11
  categories of, 12
  conversion, 11
  fixation, 10

indications:
  for analysis/therapy, 10, 13
  vs. criteria of suitability, 127
insight:
  capacity for, 14, 49, 52, 60, 100,
    127

as treatment goal, 63, 67
integrity, 20
intellectual abilities, as factor, 10, 14
    16, 49, 105, 127, 129
intensity: *see* frequency, of
    treatment sessions
interpretation(s):
    ability to use, 92, 99–101, 130,
        136
    in assessment, 29, 60
    trial, 55

Jackson, M., 115, 118, 130
Jones, E., 10, 14, 131
Joseph, B., 1, 54, 55
Joseph, E. D., 127, 128
Jung, C. G., 41, 70, 71, 78, 127, 128

Kächele, H., 128
Kantrowitz, J., 19, 20, 22, 25, 26
Karasu, T. B., 133
Kernberg, O., 16, 18, 20, 25, 34
Klauber, J., 2, 3, 4, 17, 19, 20, 21, 28,
    31, 53, 60, 61
Klein, J., 130
Kleinian meta-psychology, 83
Knapp, P. H., 19, 20, 22, 24, 59
Kohut, H., 34
Kristeva, J., 70
Kubie, L., 47, 59

Langs, R., 70, 71, 91, 125
Laufer, M., 2
Laufer, M. Eglé, 2
Lawrence, J., xiv
Leaff, L., 16, 21, 22, 29, 33
Levin, S., 19
Liberman, D., 26
libidinal development, relevance
    of, 3
life crisis, 21
Limentani, A., 16, 25, 33, 61, 64, 101
Lishman, A. L., 133
literature:
    on assessment, 7–34
    referral from, 37

Little, M., 108
Lorenz, K., 39
loss:
    defences against, 82, 84, 130
    feelings of, about assessment,
        37
    inability to bear, 130
love:
    capacity to, and psychological
        health, 4
    in infancy, role of in therapy, 1
Lower, R., 19

Mace, C., 70
Malan, D. H., 59
Malovic-Yeeles, M., xvi, 6, 125–
    134
manic-depressive psychosis, 11
    schizoid, 130
marital status, as factor, 30
Maudsley Hospital, 115
McCarter, R. H., 19
McDougall, J., 131
memories, patient's, 51
mental deficiency, 127
Modell, A., 97
moral considerations, 14
Mordecai, A., xvi, 6, 87–106
motivation, 20, 76
    role of in psychoanalysis, ix, x,
        14, 21, 27, 46, 50, 65, 68, 69,
        82
    unconscious, 136
    "will to be analysed", vs. "wish
        for recovery", 111, 112

Namnum, R., 17, 19
narcissistic character disorders, 2,
    17, 18, 21, 33, 34, 58, 135
National Health Service (NHS), 36,
    38, 40, 95
Neumann, E., 76
neurodermatitis, 44
neurosis/neuroses, 17
    age of, 14
    impulse, 11

neurosis/neuroses (*continued*)
mixed, 11
obsessional, 10, 11
transference, 21, 22, 61
vs. therapeutic alliance, 129
treatment of, 41
neurotic symptoms, 59, 63, 132

object relation(s), 21, 22, 27, 32, 75,
78, 81–84, 137
areas of, as focus of assessment,
71
in assessment setting, 19–20
core, 28
early, 19
and later therapy, 1, 3
importance of, 13, 18–20
internal, 73
patient's stage of functioning in,
4
obsessional neurosis, 10, 11
oedipal phase of development, x
vs. dyadic functioning, 4
Ogden, T., 19, 28, 60

paranoia(s), 11
paranoid–schizoid stage, 109
parental status, as factor, 30
pathologies, "of the self" and
"within the self", 129
patient:
–analyst/therapist match, 4, 9,
15, 23–26, 30, 32, 34,
128–132
history of, *see* history, patient's
memories of, *see* memories,
patient's
qualities of, 16–23
and suitability for treatment,
10–23
Pedder, J., 99
peptic ulceration, 44
perversion(s), 11, 12, 15, 17
sexual, 11
pharmacotherapies, 125

Phillips, A., 77
Pollock, G. H., 9, 25, 27, 29, 30, 104,
129
Pope, A., v
pregenital conversions, 11
primary holding, as treatment goal,
67
projection(s), 55
transference–countertransference,
72
working through, 99
projective identification, 110
psychiatric illness, as
contraindication for
psychoanalysis, 126
psychoanalysis:
aims of, 14
definition of, 8–9
suitability for, 8
literature on, 10–23
psychoanalytic abstinence, 88
psychoanalytic setting: *see* setting,
psychoanalytic
psychodynamic psychotherapy,
contraindications for,
125–134
psychological-mindedness, 4, 13,
17–18, 21, 29, 78, 127
psychology, one-person vs. two-
person, x
psychoneuroses, chronic, and
analysability, 10
psychopathology, 129
psychosis/psychoses, 10, 11, 12, 17,
115, 127, 129, 132, 136
manic-depressive, 11, 17
psychosomatic problems as
indicators for, 12
psychotherapy of, 10
psychosomatic disorders, 10, 12, 17,
44, 102, 132
psychosomatic medicine, 44
psychotherapy (*passim*):
dangers of, 132–134
vs. medicine, 5

psychoanalytic:
  aims of, 53–56
  assessment for, *passim*
  intensive, 43, 130
  literature, 7–34
  and medicine, 40
  vs. psychoanalysis, xiv
  purpose of, 48
  See also therapy
psychotic breakdown, 133
psychotic transference, 61, 130

Quinodoz, D., 94

racism, 83
reality:
  factors, 30, 89
  inner vs. outer, ability to
    distinguish between, 52,
    116, 129, 136
  testing, 16, 21
referral (*passim*):
  for assessment, 27–28
  and countertransference, 27
  family, 27
  from literature, 37
  process, 30–31
    effect of on analysis, 32
  self-, 72
  sources of, 35–46
  third-party, 76–77
  and transference, 27
regression, 17, 21, 43, 67, 130
  adaptive, 16
  capacity for, 50
  and frequency of sessions, 64
Reich, W., 10
rejection, feelings of, about
    assessment, 37
repetition compulsion, 29, 48
resistance(s), 30, 90, 92, 93, 99, 101,
    102, 104, 129
  patterns of, 27
responsibility, refusal to take, 4, 54,
    55, 131

Rey, H., 69
rheumatoid arthritis, 44
Rickman, J., x
Rosen, J., 127
Rosenfeld, H. A., 127

Sanders, K., 41
Sandler, J., 10, 11, 13, 14, 15, 18, 20,
    29, 30, 49, 59, 87, 92, 126
Sashin, J. I., 18, 19, 20
Saul, L. J., 131
schizophrenia, 11, 17, 66, 130
Schubart, W., 28, 108
screen memory, 51
Searles, H. F., 110, 127
selection, of patient–analyst match,
    128–132
self-castigation, 20
self-diagnosis, patient's, 60
self-esteem, low, 20
self-knowledge, defences against,
    54
self-reflection, capacity for, 17, 109
separation, tolerance for, 18, 21
separation anxiety, 67, 84, 130
setting:
  assessment, 6
    boundaries of, 6
    holding qualities of, 70
    object relations within, 19–23
  private, 118
  psychoanalytic, ix, 137
    holding qualities of, 67
    role of, 44
sex, as factor, 30
Shakespeare, W., v
Shapiro, S., 26, 28, 94
Simon, P., 107
Sinason, V., 129
Solomon, M., 26
somatization, 133
space, therapeutic: *see* therapeutic
    space
Steiner, J., 34, 54
Sterba, R., 131

Stone, L., 5, 8, 11, 12, 17, 19, 20, 21, 24, 28, 33, 91
story, opening, significance of, 69–85
stress:
  ability to tolerate, 133
  effects of, 43, 44
Stumpfl, M. R., xvi, 6, 107–113
stuttering, 11
sublimatory potentials, 16, 21
substance abuse, 132, 134
  See also addiction(s)
suffering, ability to tolerate, 21
suitability for treatment, 29, 59, 74, 87, 105, 136
  vs. accessibility, 128
  criteria of, 10–23, 78, 126, 127
  See also accessibility; analysability
Sullivan, H. S., 127
superego, 20, 21, 55
symbiosis, 110
Symington, N., 34

Tartakoff, H., 25
Temperley, J., 97, 137
termination, problems with, 8
terminology, limitations in, 34, 91, 126–128
therapeutic alliance, 21
  capacity to form, xi, 126, 127, 130, 133
  vs. transference neurosis, 129
therapeutic metaphors, three-stage process of meaning in, 70
therapeutic space:
  assessment as, 3, 70, 119, 122
  as holding environment, 79, 120
  use of, 6, 85
therapist:
  as blank screen, 88, 133
  fantasy of ideal, 104, 131
therapy:
  behaviour, 41, 126
  cognitive, 41

family, xi, 126
frequency of, 63–68
group, xi, 126
marital, xi, 126
pharmaco-, 125
  See also psychotherapy
Thomä, H., 128
Thompson, C., 23, 25, 30
thyrotoxicosis, 44
tics, psychogenic, 11
Tonnesmann, M., ix–xii
transference, x, 3, 6, 34, 49, 75, 91, 105, 137
  ability to use, 4, 52
  to analyst, and attachment to assessor, 2, 30
  in assessment consultation, 18, 19, 61, 107–113
  bond, positive, 11
  concept of, 98
  –countertransference:
    observations in assessment, 72
    projections, 72
  effect of assessment on, 29
  interpretations, in assessment, 29
  issues, unresolved, 133
  neurosis, 21, 22, 61
    vs. therapeutic alliance, 129
  passive dependent, 8
  patient's understanding of, 60
  phenomena, ability to deal with, 126
  psychotic, 61, 130
  reaction, infantile neurotic, 96
  and referral, 27
  relationship:
    "as if" quality of, 57, 133
    capacity to form, 32, 128
    as focus of assessment, 71
    and frequency of sessions, 67
    role of, x, 97
  true, 24
treatment alliance, 48–51, 61
  prerequisites for, 11–15, 126, 127, 129

Tyndale, A., xvi, 6, 47–61
Tyson, R. L., 10, 11, 13, 14, 15, 18,
    20, 29, 30, 49, 59, 87

ulcerative colitis, 44, 132
unconscious, the, acceptance of, 4

verbalization, capacity for, 16

Waldhorn, H. F., 15, 24, 26, 28
Waydenfeld, D., xvi, 6, 87–106
Weber, J. J., 26
Wetment, H., 19

Williams, P., 115, 118
Wilson, J., 72
Winnicott, D. W., ix, 67, 68, 91
Woolf, V., 125
work, capacity to, 21
    and psychological health, 4
working alliance, capacity for, 18
working through, 50, 55, 66
    as goal of psychoanalysis, 63
    projections/transferences, 99
    as treatment goal, 67

Zetzel, E., 8, 12, 18, 19, 20, 28, 59